Miniature

Flower Arrangements

and

Plantings

Sweet Measure of Fragrance. A flower bouquet spanned by two fingers includes lavender, verbena, alyssum, heliotrope, marigold, and thyme in a white porcelain, pedestal wine cup. Height six inches. Arrangement by the author.

Miniature Flower Arrangements and Plantings

by
Lois Wilson

Color Photographs by LOCKWOOD HAIGHT

HAWTHORN BOOKS, INC.

A Helen Van Pelt Wilson Book

PUBLISHERS NEW YORK

MINIATURE FLOWER ARRANGEMENTS AND PLANTINGS

Copyright © 1963 by Lois Wilson. Copyright under International and Pan-American Copyright Conventions. All rights reserved, including the right to reproduce this book, or portions thereof, in any form, except for the inclusion of brief quotations in a review. All inquiries should be addressed to Hawthorn Books, Inc., 70 Fifth Avenue, New York, New York 10011. This book was manufactured in the United States of America and published simultaneously in Canada by Prentice-Hall of Canada, Ltd., 1870 Birchmount Road, Scarborough, Ontario.

This is a new printing of a book originally published by D. Van Nostrand Company, Inc.

Other books by Lois Wilson

Chatelaine's Gardening Book
Flowers for Your Church
(with Adelaide B. Wilson)

Editor's Foreword

In the literature of flower arrangement there has been until this time but one area without its own book—that of the miniature. Yet tiny flower arrangements have long been a favorite type for exhibition and home decoration. Watch people at a flower show. If there are classes for miniatures, crowds will gather around them to study and enjoy their small perfection.

Wherein lies the charm of the minute? It is impossible to say, yet through the ages and over the whole world there is evidence of the appeal of small things. In this book Lois Wilson explores the history of miniatures as expressions of art and culture. She describes and illustrates toys four thousand years old—the work of ancient artists—jewelry, amulets, and mortuary figures. Many of these in replica provide accessories for today's miniature arrangements.

The craft of miniature-making is explicitly covered, and suggestions given on where to find proper in-scale plant material and also the containers that suit it. The collecting of these is presented as an exciting and fascinating hobby. Reading these chapters, we develop a new awareness, a new kind of seeing, and that surely should be one of the important results of reading any book. Thus dandelion seedlings appear as stars for a miniature Christmas scene, and an acorn cup and a boat-shaped milkweed seed pod become bowls for "mass" arrangements of tiny white violets and lily-of-the-valley buds.

Success in exhibiting is analyzed; and there are few who can speak with greater authority than Lois Wilson, who has won so many awards. She tells of the pleasure of teaching children how to find choice plants in the woods for miniature-making and how to use miniature flower arrangement, with its limited requirements of space and material, in therapy projects.

Mrs. Wilson's warm and vibrant personality and her enthusiasm shine out on every page, and I think it would be impossible to read this book and not explore at once the pleasure of making miniature flower arrangements.

HELEN VAN PELT WILSON

Preface

Who is there among us who is not fascinated by the wondrous world of tiny plants? Whether we hunt eagerly for the first purple violets of the spring or watch for the pert faces of Johnny-jump-ups to show through the soft green of our summer gardens, whether we stoop low in autumn woods to see the vivid scarlet of wintergreen berries hanging beneath their glistening leaves, there is everywhere about us through the growing year, this enchanting world of the small.

Are we not all captivated too when we see these tiny flowers and leaves lifted out of their natural setting—where nature's profusion so often disguises their true loveliness—and enhanced by deft-fingered arrangement and dainty container into a picture of tiny beauty?

To be sure, clever handling of miniature materials is not a new skill to flower lovers in this country. Here and there across the land, wherever arrangers have gathered to put on shows, or simply for their own pleasure, miniatures have had their devotees. What is new is the increasing number who now find delight in working in this small scale, in hunting for suitable materials in greenhouse and florist shop, in growing it in their own gardens, and most of all in learning to find it in the boundless world of wild plants, where the wealth of small beauty is as high as the sky, as wide as the sea, as near as your eye, as close as your hand.

These arrangers soon discover that learning to handle small-scale materials pays off a thousandfold. Dexterity with full-size flowers and foliages becomes more precise, fingers more adept than before. Judgment of what to put together, and how, is more sure, flare for dramatic contrast easier to develop. Inevitably these techniques are an excellent, refining discipline.

And as in all decorative art, the making of good miniatures leads down many other intriguing paths too. The search for beautiful little containers can be a hobby in itself, neither expensive nor unwieldy. Accessories are fun to find; they can be exquisite, humorous or clever.

Some arrangers develop a talent for making their own vases and ornaments.

Curiosity about the history of miniatures, stimulated especially by the increasing availability of good museum reproductions, opens another window on a far horizon, for there are hundreds of ways in which man has expressed his love of small things through the ages. Sculpture of little animals, flowers, and household ornaments goes back thousands of years. Illuminated manuscripts, hundreds of years old, filled with brilliantly colored, minutely detailed scenes are on view in our museums. Portraits of kings, queens, and commoners, no bigger than a locket, are other delightful miniature forms.

In addition, we have the fact that miniature flowers and plants are endearing. I have often wondered why. Perhaps as people feel more and more how wide the world is, how vast its complications, they find self-contained perfection in the small compass of a little plant? Or is it perhaps that those who grow them, those who make arrangements with them, those who come to look at them, feel in them some small miracle?

For miraculous such perfection surely is. A unique sensation comes to you as you hold one in your hand. You lift it up to see each minute and perfect detail. There passes between you and the flower and leaf a small pulse, much as you feel when you hold a dry brown seed in your hand for that moment before it is planted.

The times may be filled with terror, our own lives may be heavy with dismay or fatigue, but we take heart in this planned, treasured beauty of each flower and leaf. The pulse, the miracle, is there.

LOIS WILSON

Toronto, Canada
January, 1970

Contents

Part Four

TEACHING AND EXHIBITING WITH MINIATURES

List of Illustrations

IN COLOR

IN BLACK AND WHITE

Miniature

Flower Arrangements
and
Plantings

PART ONE

Four Thousand Years of Miniatures

1.

Miniatures in Antiquity

PEOPLE in early times were as fascinated by the making of miniatures as we are today. An Egyptian father, modeling little clay mice for his children four thousand years ago; a Chinese artist, a thousand years later, casting in bronze a handsomely decorated three-inch cauldron as an offering to his gods; a Persian painter, five hundred years ago, brilliantly illuminating manuscripts with exquisite small scenes in vermilion and gold are only three of the hundreds of thousands who have known the magnetic charm of small things, in much the same way as we who arrange miniature flowers and plants today.

Feeling this bond of similar enthusiasm, today's miniaturists are irresistibly drawn to study how these ancient artists in various media expressed delicacy and beauty. They are inspired to choose fine ornament for their own work by the form and finish of ancient small figures, often using reproductions of them as determining accessories for their arrangements. From artifacts in museums they gather new ideas for exciting shapes in containers which many of them then make by hand. Learning how Persian illuminators handled perspective is only one of the lessons which helps them to be more aware of the pos-

(1) (2)

(3) (4)

ILLUSTRATIONS 1–4. REPRODUCTIONS OF ANCIENT PIECES

1. Three Gerboa Mice more than four thousand years old, made of faience (clay), about two inches high. Original in The Metropolitan Museum of Art, Carnarvon Collection, Gift of Edward S. Harkness. 2. Figure of a Horse from the third century, B.C., Chinese, Han Dynasty, cast in bronze. Height three and one quarter inches, length three and one-eighth inches, without base. Original also from The Metropolitan Museum of Art. Gift of George D. Pratt, 1928. (Replicas of both available from The Museum.) 3. Peacock Gold Weight in bronze used by the Ashanti Tribe of the Gold Coast, West Africa, to weigh gold dust. Two inches high. Original in Wurtzburger Collection, Baltimore, Maryland. 4. Candleholder, originally a carved wooden pipe bowl made by the Tlingit Indians of Southern Alaska, at one end a bear sitting on another bear's head, at the other, a bird. Late nineteenth century. Four inches high. Original in The American Museum of Natural History. (Both reproduced by Alva Museum Replicas, Inc., New York)

sibilities of exploiting in their own designs the dimension of depth as well as of width and height. In fact, everything in this field of study can be usefully applied to the making of finer miniatures.

SMALL ANIMAL FIGURES

We know that small figures of animals have always been a popular miniature form, for they have been found in archeological digs of many periods and all over the world. Used as offerings for gods, in animal-increase rites, as amulets or charms, for jewelry, seals, weights for gold, and everywhere, as one would expect, as toys for children, these small figures in clay, bronze, and even precious gold, silver, ivory, and jade can be seen in every good museum collection in the world.

Three of the most enchanting are the trio of Gerboa Mice in the collection of the Metropolitan Museum of Art in New York. Tiny creatures, not two inches high, they were found in the Delta area of Egypt and date back nearly four thousand years. They were modeled from the Gerboa mouse, a little animal with kangaroolike hind legs that inhabits Egypt's desert fringe, where on moonlight nights they leap and dance in little bands. Inexpensively reproduced and available through the Museum, they would make delightful accessories for a child's garden or an arrangement of small grains and grasses (Illustration 1).

Even smaller than the mice are some of the animal figures used in ancient jewelry and as amulets. An Egyptian necklace, now in the Metropolitan Museum, has nine polychrome faience kittens, all seated in the same pose, but each slightly different from the other. Only three quarters of an inch high, they date from the time of Ptolemy, about fifteen hundred years before the birth of Christ. This section of the Museum also has a captivating collection of animal charms and seals. All are an inspiration to discriminating collectors of accessories (Illustration 5).

Thousands of miles away from Egypt, and yet still of the same period in time, small bronze animals, sculptured with lively character, have been found in the tombs of the Far East. One of the best of these, a bronze horse of the Han dynasty, less than four inches high, is fortunately now reproduced and available through the Metropolitan Mu-

(5)

(6)

(7)

ILLUSTRATIONS 5–7. ANCIENT ARTIFACTS

5. Miniature Kittens from an Egyptian necklace almost three thousand years old. Made of faience, a kind of clay, and multicolored, each just three-quarters of an inch high. The Metropolitan Museum of Art, New York. 6. Classical Antiquities. Antique glass vials and bottles, originally used to hold precious oil and other liquids. Less than five inches. The Metropolitan Museum of Art, New York. Gift of J. Pierpont Morgan, 1917. 7. Egyptian Amulets, worn as charms or used as seals, and often in the form of animals. From left to right, an ape, a sow, a ram, a monkey, a hare, a hedgehog, and a shrew; approximately three thousand years old and made of faience. The Metropolitan Museum of Art, New York.

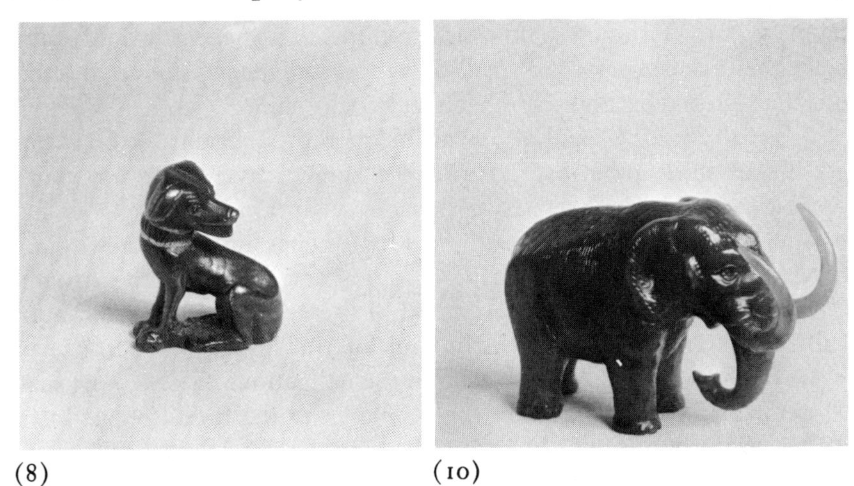

(8) (10)

(9)

ILLUSTRATIONS 8–10. THREE MINIATURE ANIMALS

8. Figure of a Dog with a gold collar, this could represent a modern pet, but he is more than three thousand years old and Egyptian. The Metropolitan Museum of Art, New York. Rogers Fund, 1947. 9. Figure of a Cat in blue faience with black spots, Egyptian, nearly four thousand years old, found in a grave in Matarieh. Two and three-eighths inches long. The Metropolitan Museum of Art, New York. Carnarvon Collection. Gift of Edward S. Harkness, 1926. 10. Figure of the Hairy Mammoth of Siberia, a nineteenth century Russian carving, sculptured delicately in nephrite. The Metropolitan Museum of Art, New York. Gift of Heber R. Bishop, 1902.

seum of Art. With his stocky body and merry stance, he would make a delightful accessory for a small flower arrangement planned to bring out the spirit of his high-held head and cocky tail.

Equally useful—and also available as reproductions—are a Tlingit Indian stone pipe in the form of a young raven with its mouth open, three and a half inches high; a Peruvian pottery vessel showing two monkeys side by side, four and a half inches high; and a two-inch bronze gold weight in the shape of a peacock, made by the Ashanti Tribe of the African Gold Coast. All of these little figures are beautifully made and finished with the look of the silver, gold, bronze or stone of the originals. The raven is in the collections of The American Museum of Natural History, the monkeys in the Smithsonian Institution at Washington D.C. and the peacock in the Wurtzberger Collection in Baltimore, Maryland.

Also in collections on this continent and in the Far East are small sculptures called *netsukes*, little ornaments carved of fine materials and worn with Japanese ceremonial dress in the eighteenth and nineteenth centuries. They acted as a toggle fastened at the end of a cord that, at its other end, was threaded through a beautiful little snuff or medicine case and was tucked into the sash at the waist. Some of the most engaging are miniatures of animals, birds, and fish. A few lucky arrangers have been acquiring these bewitching little figures to use as accessories with interpretative classes in flower shows or as small ornaments to complement Japanese arrangements.

TREASURES FROM ANCIENT GRAVES

The use of miniatures as offerings to the gods has been widespread for hundreds of years. Placed most often in graves because people believed that the spirits of the dead could take such things with them, they ranged from a piece as delicate as a carved ivory trinket box to something as practical as a cooking pot.

The ivory jewel box, only a few inches high, was found in a woman's chamber tomb on the north slope of the Areopagus in Greece by the American School of Classical Studies. It is covered with the most intricately carved pattern of griffons chasing a deer and the fitted lid also is highly ornamented. The cooking pot, in the Far Eastern collection of the Royal Ontario Museum in Toronto, is less

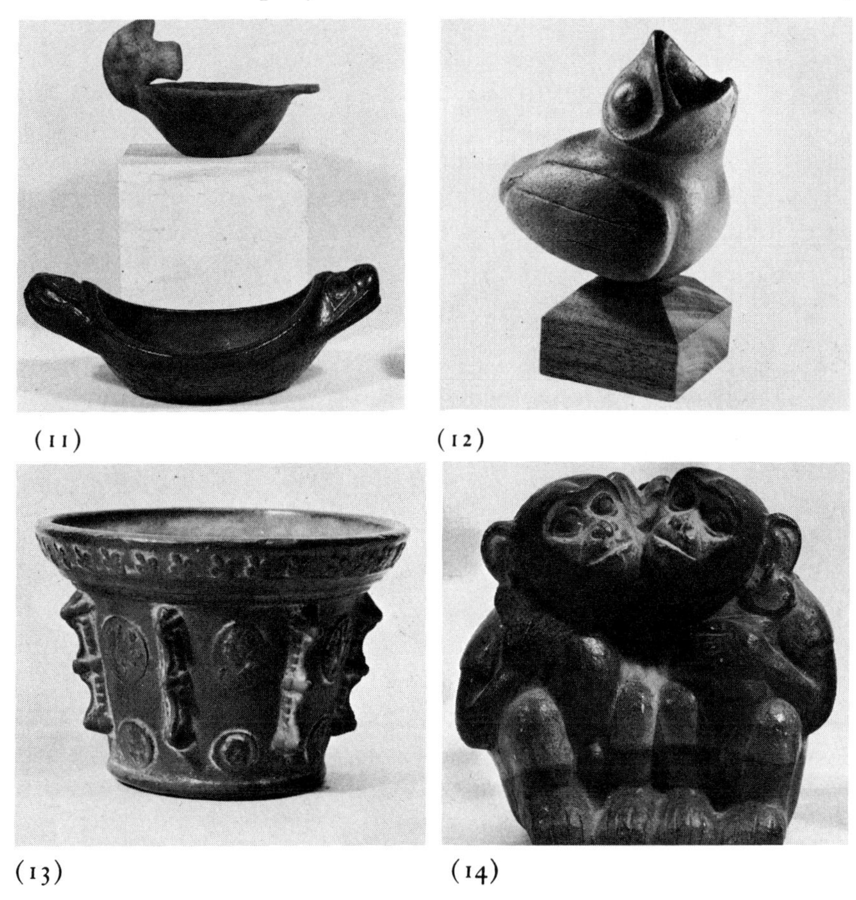

(11) (12)

(13) (14)

ILLUSTRATIONS 11–14. REPRODUCTIONS OF ORIGINALS IN AMERICAN MUSEUMS

11. American Indian Effigy Bowl of pottery with the figure of an animal on the rim; about eight hundred years old. Three and three quarter inches high. Original in Smithsonian Institution, Washington, D.C. Feast or Oil Dish carved in wood by the Tlingit Indians of Alaska. Original in Buffalo Museum of Science, Buffalo, N.Y. 12. Young Raven with Open Mouth. The original of this piece is a stone pipe carved by the Tlingit Indians in the nineteenth century. Three and one half inches high. Original in American Museum of Natural History, N.Y. 13. Seventeenth century Italian Mortar, decorated with motifs inspired by coins and cameos, four inches high, six inches in diameter. Original in Baltimore Museum of Art, Baltimore, Cone Collection. 14. Pottery Vessel with Two Monkeys from the North Coast of Peru. Intended to hold liquid, it had ceremonial use and was buried with the dead. Four and one half inches high, probably more than a thousand years old. Original in Smithsonian Institution, Washington, D.C. These reproductions are the exact size of the originals and are suitable for containers and available from Alva Museum Replicas, Inc., New York.

(15)

(16)

ILLUSTRATIONS 15, 16. JAPANESE IVORIES

15. Ivory Case, highly decorated, used by the Japanese in the nineteenth century to carry medicine or snuff. The case itself or *inro* is painted in delicate colors; the cord from which it hung is held by an *ojime*—in this case an agate bead—and by the *netsuke*, a carved ornament which kept the *inro* from slipping out from under the belt. This *netsuke* is beautifully inlaid with mother-of-pearl. The Metropolitan Museum of Art, New York. Bequest of Mrs. H. O. Havemeyer, 1929, the H. O. Havemeyer Collection. 16. Netsukes. The top row of octopuses; the middle row, left to right, a little bear, a rabbit, and a baby bird; the bottom row, a string of mushrooms. The Metropolitan Museum of Art, New York. Bequest of Edward C. Moore, 1891.

(17)

ILLUSTRATION 17. IVORY JEWEL BOX

A rare small piece intricately carved, of the Mycenaean period—fourteenth century, B.C. Agora Excavations, American School of Classical Studies, Athens, Greece.

than four inches high. Dated in the Shang Dynasty, it is a most beautifully proportioned small piece. Two-handled, banded with a delicate pattern of spirals and circles, and with two ear loop handles at the sides, it stands on three small legs about an inch high. Time has added a finish of soft green overlay to the dark strength of the bronze. Both this bronze and the Greek ivory are more than three thousand years old.

Also in this category of "mortuary offerings," as they are officially called, are small vases and miniatures of household ornament found in ancient graves. These pieces, again only a few inches high or wide, have lovely proportions and although the finish is often coarse, many, like the T'ang group in Illustration 19, show a soft, creamy glaze that would be a perfect foil for flowers and leaves. As we picture these little vases in their own time so many centuries ago, we wonder if they may not have held small bouquets of fragrant flowers and herbs before their proper use, and also perhaps at the time of their burial.

(18)

ILLUSTRATION 18. BRONZE TING

Three-legged cauldron of the Shang Dynasty in China, more than three thousand years old. Probably made as a burial offering. The Royal Ontario Museum, Toronto, Canada. Gift of the Flavelle Foundation.

GOLD AND ENAMELED LANDSCAPES IN EGYPT

The Egyptians loved flowers. Archaeologists find evidence of their use in that country in bowls as decoration, as garlands worn by guests at parties and, more interesting still, as inspiration for the making of miniature gold and brightly enameled landscapes. In *Period Flower Arrangement* (Barrows), Margaret Marcus tells of these tiny precious gardens made usually for a cherished gift or as a commission for a wealthy person. They would represent, in the finest materials and with the most exquisite workmanship, little formal gardens with flowers, walks, pavilions, and even birds among the flowers. They were also sometimes a miniature desert landscape with African huts and tropical trees with monkeys playing in them. What an interesting hobby for someone with a talent for making both jewelry and landscape designs!

FAR EASTERN BURIAL FIGURES

About the tenth century, A.D., we find miniature burial figures of the Far East telling another fascinating story of how people lived. At first, because men believed that they could take with them into the afterlife some of the comforts and conveniences of this one, their wives, servants, and household animals were killed and buried with them when they died. Eventually small clay models replaced the living sacrifices.

Excavations for highways, dams, and railways, and planned archeological expeditions have uncovered many of these furnished graves, some with dozens of small figures. Although China does not permit their export now, in years past many complete burial processions, and some single figures as well, were shipped out of the country and now form valuable exhibits in museums in the Western world.

Although most of these miniature burial figures and their reproductions are larger than the scale we use in miniature flower arrangements today, the interest in them is growing and we hope that it will be possible soon to get smaller sizes, for they have a special appeal to the arranger conscious of bringing to her work the most lovely ornament of other crafts, both ancient and modern.

ILLUMINATED MANUSCRIPTS AND ALBUMS

Although today we use the word "miniature" to describe anything that is a small reproduction of something larger, the word is really derived from the Latin *minium.* Minium was the vermilion used on borders of pages and as one of the brilliant colors in tiny pictorial scenes painted around initials in illuminated manuscripts and musical scores for the thirteen hundred years between the fourth and seventeenth century A.D. In Illustration 21, we show a Venetian miniature of the early fifteenth century, now in the Metropolitan Museum

(19)

(20)

ILLUSTRATIONS 19, 20. CHINESE TREASURES FROM THE PAST

19. T'ang Stoneware Vases, more than a thousand years old found in graves in China, a stem cup probably used in ceremonies, a tiny basket with a twisted handle and floral decorations, and a pierced base for a larger cup, all covered with a transparent glaze. 20. Chinese Porcelain Household Utensils of the Ch'ing Dynasty, seventeenth and eighteenth centuries. Left, a yellow-glazed sake cup, less than two inches high, with a decoration of dragons on the outside and on the handles, one of which has been broken. Center, Blue-and-White Honey Pot, with design of landscape and figures and thunder pattern collar on the body, two and five-eighths inches high. Right, Ceremonial Cup, the shape copied from those made of rhinoceros horn, this one in Fukien ware. All from The Royal Ontario Museum, Toronto, Canada.

of Art, done in this fashion in gold leaf and tempera on parchment. Only a few inches high, it is a delicately beautiful painting of the Virgin and Child seated amid a stylized pattern of graceful leaves and flowers.

Such manuscripts, lettered and illustrated by the most skilful artists, were the picture books of their day. The twelfth-century Winchester Bible, now in the Cathedral Library in Winchester, England, is one of the most fascinating pieces of illumination that has been preserved. Lettered by hand on vellum, the finely worked illustration around many of the initials, includes the special plants and flowers of the Bible. One, in the book of *Jeremiah*, Folio 148, shows an intricate design of the prophet surrounded by a stylized grape vine, the symbol of peace and abundance in Biblical times and the plant to which Jesus compared himself, with his disciples as the branches (Illustration 22).

Illuminations for such manuscripts took years to complete. Illustrations for the famous *Dastan-i-Amir Hamza*, a popular romance story of Moghul times in India, were worked on for fifteen years and by a number of different artists. In addition to the vermilion color which gives miniatures their name, these illuminations were often heavily painted with silver and gold. The story is told of one band of persecuting Arabs who burned fourteen sacks of Manichean manuscripts until trickles of gold and silver ran out of the burning paintings into the fire.

Such ornate illustration of manuscripts was also popular in Persia for hundreds of years. Because the Persians loved flowers and gardens, much of the decorative detail surrounding the figures in these little scenes included stylized trees, repeating patterns of branches, vines and leaves and, through all, brightly colored birds. To us today, these pictures, which can be seen in the great public art collections, have a fairy-tale quality.

Perhaps the greatest glory of miniature illustration came in India under the art-loving Moghul emperors of the seventeenth century. As in Persia, the most widely appreciated works of this period were pictures of flowers and trees with birds. The Moghul school was also especially skilful in creating, in the small space of a painting, the illusion of distance and of three dimensions in a two-dimensional form. The designs had as well a remarkable continuity and flow of line.

To create a feeling of distance, Moghul artists used a receding

(21) (22)

ILLUSTRATIONS 21, 22. ILLUMINATED INITIALS

21. Initial with Virgin and Child. This delicate painting, only a few inches high, illuminates a Venetian musical manuscript of the early fifteenth century. The Metropolitan Museum of Art, New York, Rogers Fund, 1912. 22. An illuminated letter from the book of *Jeremiah*, in the Winchester Bible. The Dean and Chapter of Winchester, Winchester Cathedral Library, Winchester, England.

background, particularly at the horizon of a landscape. They also introduced for the first time in this medium, the distant view of figures and animals to give a sense of depth. We employ these techniques in arrangements, both full-size and miniature, when we create the illusion of distance by careful placement of materials.

Both Persian and Indian miniaturists often used stylized borders of vines and leaves. Within these the design was broken into a number of small spaces, each with its own scene but with a connecting design of flowing lines in branches, vines, gesture, posture, or folds in robes. This movement of rhythmic line through a composition has also been a familiar principle in good arrangement. A study of these illuminated manuscripts to discover how this has been accomplished in such small scale can be particularly useful to the flower arranger who wishes to improve her own skill by such devices.

(23)

ILLUSTRATION 23. PERSIAN MINIATURE

From a manuscript of the *Bustan* by Saidi of the Bokhara School, this shows the Sultan of Syria, Melik-i-Saleh, interviewing two dervishes. Painted in the sixteenth century, this little scene illustrates the Persian love of flowers, plants and birds and the intricate handling of perspective and complex design. The Metropolitan Museum of Art, New York, Hewitt Fund, 1911.

(24)

ILLUSTRATION 24. MODERN PERSIAN MINIATURE

Painted on the lid of a silver box in the highly ornamented style of the early Persian portraits. Stylized vines, flowers, and leaves frame the portrait of a beautiful lady of the court. *The Globe and Mail*, Toronto, Canada.

MINIATURE PORTRAITS

As printing developed, the practice of illumining manuscripts gradually declined. Artists turned to the problems of fidelity in painting people. They painted the whole figure first, then began to concentrate on the head. Thus the portrait miniature emerged. It reached a particularly high standard with the work of Hans Holbein, the

Younger, in the sixteenth century. From then on, particularly in England, many brilliant artists specialized in this small-scale painting.

Most miniature portraits were designed to be keepsakes and were given to friends and family as we give photographs today. King James I of England, the story goes, once rewarded sixteen of his courtiers at one time with "cheynes with his picture hanging by the valewe of some thyrty or forty pounde." Nicholas Hillyarde, court miniaturist to King James, was the artist of this generous commission. The most famous of the great group of Elizabethan miniaturists, Hillyarde, like Durer and Holbein whom he admired and copied, was trained as a goldsmith as well as a painter. One often sees, in the frames of the miniatures of this period, exquisite work with filigree, rubies, emeralds, sapphires and pearls reflecting this auxiliary talent of the painter.

Miniatures were painted with opaque colors, first on backgrounds of playing cards, sometimes just on a piece of chicken skin wetted and stretched across stiff paper. Eventually they developed into the delicate pieces of ivory, painted with clear colors and beautifully framed, that we see in museum and gallery collections today. The work of the most famous of the European miniaturists forms a virtually unbroken line of excellence for over three centuries, and when "miniature painting" came to America, artists here carried on with a comparable, if plainer, quality. Photography has today taken over from the painter in this art, yet it seems a pity that there is now little opportunity for the painter of miniature portraits. Even the earliest in our collections have a poignant beauty seldom seen in photographs today.

PORCELAINS AND IVORIES

Just as the portrait painters of Europe and America sought through the years to refine materials and techniques, the craftsmen in other miniature media also learned the secrets of making more beautiful pieces. By the eighteenth century in the Ch'ing Dynasty, small ceramics were being made with the greatest delicacy and grace. Even household pieces such as saki cups were designed with exquisite pierced handles. A white-lidded honey pot would be decorated with a tiny, bright blue landscape and finely drawn small figures under a high glaze. A fine milk-white porcelain cup in Fukien ware, copied

(25) (26) (27) (28)

ILLUSTRATIONS 25–28. MINIATURE PORTRAITS

25. French miniature portrait of Augusta Temple Prime. A delicate water color on ivory painted by the French Miniaturist Isabey in the early nineteenth century. The Metropolitan Museum of Art, New York. Gift of Cornelia Prime, 1908. 26. German miniature, *Man in a Red Cap* by Hans Holbein, the Younger. Painted in the early sixteenth century in tempera and oil on wood. The Metropolitan Museum of Art, New York. Bequest of Mary Stillman Harkness, 1950. 27. American miniature, *Portrait of a Child*, by an unknown American artist of the early nineteenth century on ivory. Simple by European standards, this little picture is full of character. The Metropolitan Museum of Art, New York. Fletcher Fund, 1935. 28. British miniature, *Portrait of a Lady*, supposedly Catherine Charlotte de la Tremoille, Princesse de Condé, wife of Henri I de Bourbon, by Nicholas Hillyarde, the most famous of the English miniaturists. Dated 1597, it is done in gouache on paper. The Metropolitan Museum of Art, New York.

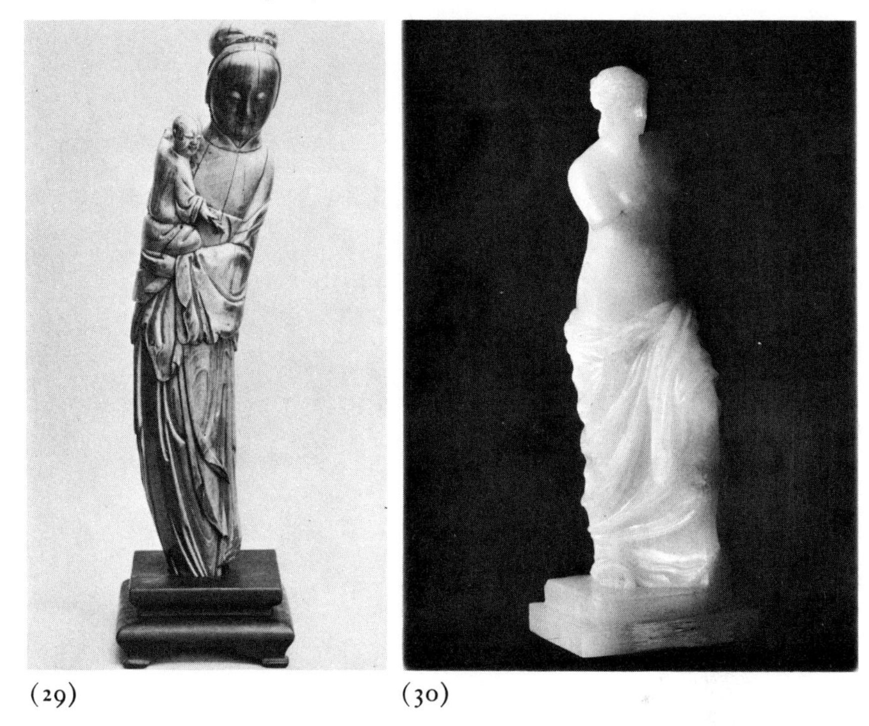

(29) (30)

ILLUSTRATIONS 29, 30. SCULPTURE IN MINIATURE

29. Chinese Mother and Child, an ivory statuette of the seventeenth or eighteenth century, the posture beautifully handled with characteristic draping of the robe. The Metropolitan Museum of Art, New York, Rogers Fund, 1913. 30. Statuette of Venus de Milo exquisitely carved in jadeite. French, nineteenth century, a little over three and one half inches high. The Metropolitan Museum of Art, New York. Gift of Heber R. Bishop, 1902.

from the cherished rhinoceros horn ceremonial cup, would have an intricate relief decoration of a goat, a crane, a crab, and pine branches (Illustration 20).

Sculptors using fine materials created such lovely pieces as the ivory statuette of K'ang Hsi mother and child and the Venus de Milo of French jade, both in the Metropolitan Museum of Art (Illustrations 29 and 30). The arranger of miniatures who takes time to study such beautiful pieces as these will be inspired to seek similar lovely accessories to set off her own work.

2.

Modern Miniatures

WE know that in years gone by the magnetism of miniatures was strong, but we know too that here and now artists are creating in various media small-scaled objects of great beauty, with a dedication as keen as that of any craftsman of old.

THE THORNE ROOMS IN CHICAGO

In America, we have a unique link between present and past in the amazing Thorne Rooms, now among the permanent exhibits of the Art Institute of Chicago. These rooms, designed and produced by Mrs. James Ward Thorne, are reproductions or reconstructions of famous examples of the best of European and American decoration. The rooms are built to a scale of one inch to the foot, making them one twelfth the size of the original.

With brilliant skill Mrs. Thorne has created in a three-sided space, hardly twenty-four inches wide, the historic style and dramatic appeal of sixty-seven different rooms as they might have appeared in Europe and America over the last four hundred years. Her solution of the problem of scale is remarkable, with each piece of furniture,

(31)

ILLUSTRATION 31. MINIATURE DESK

Decorated with a tiny bowl of tulips, this desk sits in the Queen Anne Library of the Thorne Rooms. Spectacles indicate the scale. Thorne European Rooms in Miniature, The Art Institute of Chicago.

fabric, and ornament related to produce consistent beauty. Her first rooms were entirely furnished with miniature pieces she picked up in her travels. The occasional book on table or chair came from a unique English collection in which even the text is in scale. Later Mrs. Thorne decided that much of what she needed would have to be made to her own specifications. Special processes were developed to obtain a hairline fineness in moldings and ornament, and textiles were made that exactly reproduced originals. Most of the rugs were woven under her direction by the Needlework and Textile Guild of Chicago.

Elizabethan portraits and suits of armor only inches high decorate a Tudor Great Hall. Sconces, chandeliers and candlesticks through all the rooms give make-believe light. A Welsh cupboard with one-inch pewter plates and steins stands against the wall of an eighteenth-

(32)

ILLUSTRATION 32. ENTRANCE HALL AND STAIRWAY, ENGLAND, 1775

A dainty bouquet on the console table picks up the flowery theme of the arabesques on the walls and the little Wedgwood cameos in the sconces. Thorne European Rooms in Miniature, The Art Institute of Chicago.

century English cottage. There is even a three-inch rubber plant at the heavily draped window of a nineteenth-century New York parlor.

Any room which in its own day would have had bowls or vases of flowers is decorated with them in the Thorne Rooms, all exquisitely made and perfectly colored. A miniature comport of garden flowers, less than two inches high stands on a piano in a Georgian drawing room of the Sheraton period in England. A bowl of tulips, smaller than the width of the lens in your reading glasses, is set on an eighteenth-century English library desk. A typical English garden bouquet in an entrance hall in Adam style repeats the flowery arabesques on the walls, and a pair of porcelain bowls on side tables in the dining room of a Jeffersonian house of 1800 hold arrangements of full-blown single peonies in the same tiny scale. Even the most modern of the American set, a hallway of a penthouse apartment in San Francisco, has a perfectly placed contemporary line arrangement of tropical foliage in a Chinese bowl on a carved wood base.

You could search the world over and never find so inspiring an example of miniature work as the Thorne Rooms, nor so marvellous a lesson in the handling of all parts of the whole in perfect scale to create the ultimate in beauty.

BONSAI—THE DWARF TREES IN JAPAN

Equally inspiring, but in the realm of live plants and therefore bridging the old skills of the miniature with the new, are the bonsai, the dwarf trees of Japan. Some fifteen hundred years ago, the Japanese began to collect naturally stunted trees that they found in the wild, transplanting them to beautiful containers and placing them in their gardens for daily enjoyment. The sight of a finely trained, two-foot model of a full-size tree reminded them of the natural beauty of the forest and gave opportunity for that serene contemplation of nature, so highly valued in their culture.

By the end of the sixteenth century, an art had grown up around the handling of these natural trees, as growers worked to improve them and to compensate for any natural defects. Thus was developed the art of bonsai, the disciplining and training of dwarf trees as we now know it.

In the beginning, the ownership of a bonsai was the mark of an

(33)

ILLUSTRATION 33. SHERATON DRAWING ROOM, 1800

A comport of flowers stands on the harpsichord, picking up the pattern of needle-point screen. Thorne European Rooms in Miniature, The Art Institute of Chicago.

(34)

ILLUSTRATION 34. JEFFERSONIAN DINING ROOM, 1800

Single white peonies on a side table contribute to the gracious beauty of the miniature of a home in Virginia at the turn of the nineteenth century. Thorne American Rooms in Miniature, The Art Institute of Chicago.

aristocrat. Good specimens were expensive and those most treasured were stunted naturally and therefore originally valuable, in addition to the care given after they were collected. Because such stunted trees were scarce, and high in cost, ingenious bonsai fanciers eventually developed ways in their own nurseries and gardens, of creating the look of a naturally stunted bonsai from normal stock. It still took months, even years, to grow a perfect tree, but to the grower all stages were both beautiful and exciting. Gardeners in every country will understand this excitement, for to them also there is beauty in every aspect of a plant's growth.

For many years the secrets of growing bonsai were jealously guarded and passed on only by master to pupil, father to son. Many of the most treasured specimens became family heirlooms. Hundred-year-old bonsai are common in Japan today and we hear of a five-needled pine in Tokyo's Imperial Palace that is more than three hundred years old. Those of us who have ever tried to keep a few geraniums alive over a winter or an African violet flowering on a kitchen window sill acknowledge the measure of such patient skill.

There is today a growing interest in all the garden arts of Japan, and many gardeners, particularly in America, are eager to learn how to grow and train bonsai. One of the finest collections on this continent can be seen at The Brooklyn Botanic Garden in New York, and their handbook, *Dwarfed Potted Trees* is available by mail from the Garden. Other excellent books on bonsai are listed in the Bibliography.

Florists and nursery suppliers in some of the large cities of the United States and Canada are now handling started bonsai, and at least one nursery, in San Francisco, grows and sells large specimens which have had their early training under the skilful fingers of professional bonsai-growers in Japan. While visiting this nursery two years ago, I saw their magnificent collection. A few had been started in the nursery from cuttings, but the most picturesque had been imported from Japan, bare root, as plant importation laws demand. They had then been potted up, and well cared for over the two to three years required for them to recover from the shock of transplanting and shipping.

As we walked about the nursery it was fascinating to see the owner automatically picking needles and tufts from his specimens as he talked. Needle pruning, he said, was an almost constant business.

(35)

(36)

ILLUSTRATIONS 35, 36. BONSAI FROM THE BROOKLYN BOTANIC GARDEN

35. A Trident Maple, *Acer buergerianum*, seventy-five years old, but only two feet high and three feet wide, sent in 1961 as a gift from the City of Tokyo to the City of New York. Wire supports anchoring it to the pan through drainage holes in the bottom will be removed after one year, and replaced when the tree gets its three- to four-year root pruning and transplanting. 36. Japanese Dwarf White Pine, *Pinus parviflora*, thirty to forty years old, also sent in 1961. Multistemmed, it grows in moss-covered soil on a rock slab. Looking like a giant of the north woods it is, in actual fact, only twenty-eight inches high and three feet at the widest spread. The Brooklyn Botanic Garden, Brooklyn, New York. The Holsten Collection.

When you see the open, rhythmic line of his lovely small trees, you can understand why this is true for, allowed to develop naturally, they would have grown thick and clumsy. Looking at the windswept tiny pines, the tufted larches, the little crabapples hung with bright fruit, I inquired what the most popular variety was with his American customers. "Oh, everybody wants blue spruce," he said. Although I was horrified at first, for I think of a spruce tree as being most beautiful when it is a symmetrical triangle, a blue spruce properly trained does make a very interesting bonsai cascade.

MAME OR BABY BONSAI

Even more interesting to present-day miniature enthusiasts is the more recent work of a few people in Japan in the growing of *mame* or baby bonsai. Where the usual bonsai is about two feet high and two feet wide, there are three classes of bonsai even smaller. The *katate-mochi* about one foot high can be carried in one hand. This size is often seen as a temporary ornament on a desk, for to be healthy, it can only be kept indoors for only a few hours and then must be put outside again. A smaller size is nicknamed "baby bonsai" or mame. Usually about two and a half inches high, it can be placed in the palm of the hand. There are smaller ones still, the pygmy *shito-bonsai*, so tiny they can be carried on the tip of a finger. The pots used for these are no bigger than half of a walnut shell (Color Plates 3 and 4).

The hazards of daily life, one would think, would be almost more than such a tender little thing could survive, yet there are *shito-bonsai* in Japan today that are already scores of years old.

THE NAKAMURA COLLECTION OF MAME BONSAI

One of Japan's outstanding comedians of theatre and moving pictures, Zeko Nakamura, is famous also as a grower of baby bonsai (Illustration 39). Because he has no garden space, he grows hundreds of miniature bonsai on his roof in Tokyo. In the Brooklyn Botanic Garden's Handbook, *Dwarfed Potted Trees*, Mr. Nakamura says that on a warm, summer day when he is playing in a theatre in the center of Tokyo, between the acts he will often go home, three and a half

(37)

(38)

ILLUSTRATIONS 37, 38. MAME BONSAI TRAINED BY FRANK OKAMURA

37. Dwarf Boxwood seven years old, moss retinosporas, three years and six years. 38. Rockspray five years old, evergreen honeysuckle three years, moss retinospora, five years, Monterey cypress, four years. These specially made containers, glazed in soft colors outside, unglazed inside, and with drainage hole, are available from the Garden. The Brooklyn Botanic Garden, Brooklyn, New York.

miles away, to pour cool water on his tiny plants, for they must never dry out even if they have to be watered two or three times a day in hot weather. If he must be away from home, his family takes care of his precious collection with, as he says, "interest and pleasure for it takes five to ten years to produce a baby bonsai worthy of the name or fit to be admired."

Such devotion and patience would be rare among miniature plant lovers in this country, yet we can learn, and perhaps copy in a small way, the principles of design and care that make baby bonsai beautiful.

CULTURE OF MAME BONSAI

The beauty of mame bonsai depends as much on a lovely and properly made container as on the little plant growing in it. Small containers, made especially, are available in half a dozen shapes from the Brooklyn Botanic Garden in New York. Each is glazed in a soft color on the outside, but with the porous clay left bare on the inside and on the bottom, and with a drainage hole in the base. For arrangers who are accomplished potters as well, the making of such attractive small containers for the growing of miniature plants like baby bonsai can be fascinating.

Material suitable for such plantings is not easy to find. I have had the best results by cutting a shapely, small branch off a large bush or tree like Korean box or chamaecyparis, rooting and then potting it. Other collectors of mame bonsai have had good luck and great fun with seedlings found in the wild, particularly in cracks in rocks, crevices and windswept places where nourishment is scanty and the buffeting of wind severe. Equally interesting but much longer in producing a plant of seeable size is the growing of baby bonsai from seed; there are many miniature admirers who would find great pleasure this way.

The care of mame bonsai is demanding, especially as to moisture. They must be watered every day, even in winter, and on hot days perhaps five or six times. Soil is a mixture of clay and topsoil with a highly diluted fertilizer added rarely. Sharp drainage is encouraged because thus the soil stays sweet.

Plants are grown in full sun, exposed to storm and rain and only

(39)

ILLUSTRATION 39. ZEKO NAKAMURA

The famous Japanese actor and movie star prunes a favorite mame bonsai at his home in Tokyo.

brought in to a cool but non-freezing temperature during the winter to prevent the breaking of containers by frost and soil expansion inside. If they are brought indoors at any time to be admired, it is only for a few hours. They are then returned to garden shelves or tables where they remain for the rest of the year.

Root pruning, wiring for form, and pruning of branches goes on, just as in the training of full-size bonsai, with the most beautiful plants gradually taking the shape of the forest or garden tree of which they are a miniature.

BONKEI—TRAY LANDSCAPES WITH PLANTS

The Japanese are indeed masters of many things miniature, but none more delightful than their tray landscapes or bonkei. These are three-dimensional reproductions of beautiful scenes that in nature would extend for miles. Usually no more than two feet by one and only a few inches deep, through careful scaling of material, they give a sense of great distance (Color Plates 5 and 6).

In Japan today, there are more than a dozen schools teaching the techniques of bonkei to hundreds of interested pupils of all ages, many of them studying for years to perfect the art. The making of bonkei begins with a beautiful container, usually pottery in a soft color, sometimes glazed. Metal, wood and concrete can also be used. The main bold line of the landscape is a mountain or rocky outcropping, made traditionally with natural rock which has been collected for the purpose. The Japanese have always found symbolism in stones and many specimens have been treasured in the same family for years, often with beautifully carved stands made specially for them.

Toward the end of the nineteenth century (the earliest records of bonkei go back to the fourteenth), bonkei increased greatly in popularity. At that time, it was found that *keto* peat could be substituted for rock, then becoming scarce. This peat can be kneaded and sculptured into various forms and when well soaked with water it is also a medium for keeping growing plants like dwarf trees alive.

After the peat is molded and the miniature trees planted in it, the surface is coated with *hena-tsuchi* clay. After this dries, it is painted to resemble the surface of the ground. Moss, either as it is naturally gathered or dried and sieved, is then sprinkled over the clay to give a textured surface. Sand is added to denote the sea or a stream, and water is poured over it until it is wet and flat. If the bonkei is to be an ocean scene, little spindrifts of white sand are dribbled over the dark sand to suggest waves. Small figures, garden ornaments, buildings or boats are sometimes added for further interest and to indicate the scale of the scene.

Each little garden gives a sense of season. The two which we illustrate were made especially for us by Koshu Oyama of the Oyama School in Tokyo. Both show the brilliant colors of autumn foliage with a few deciduous trees bare and the ground covered with fallen leaves. All within the measure of a two-foot tray, we have a peaceful, timely garden scene with a little stream bubbling from the rocks, a stone lantern and a well with tiny hens and chickens pecking beside it, a garden fence and open gate and, softening all, fine specimens of miniature evergreens and leafy trees.

The second bonkei is a model of one of the eight famous beauty spots near Lake Biwa. A little hut on a hill and rocky outcroppings frame the view of mountains and lake in the distance, with low trees of bright orange and scarlet among the evergreens. A tiny figure of a kimono-clad lady walks over the swept ground in front of the hut. Students in bonkei schools in Japan are encouraged to reproduce in miniature such beautiful scenes as this, and their copybooks frequently include sketches of them to suggest exercises for practice at home.

We of the Western world often wonder what it is that draws a Japanese to such painstaking work. The clue may perhaps be found in a remark by one of their masters, "With a little practice, you can create in a few minutes right in your own home, charming sceneries which relieve the longing to be near nature and to enjoy it in the midst of the bursting city."

These little landscapes, which take a trained student only about an hour to prepare, last on the average for ten days. There is study now going on in Japan to devise ways to make them last longer. With artificial material this would not be difficult, but to those who love growing things, the loss of living trees and plants from bonkei would be a sad price to pay for longer life. In a sense, we of the West create our own kind of bonkei when we plant a berry bowl or dish garden, but we do not usually attempt to recreate the sense of distance and dimension of Japanese bonkei-makers.

BONSEKI—TRAY LANDSCAPES WITH ROCKS AND SAND

Also a landscape made on a tray, bonseki differ from bonkei in that they include no plant material, only stones and sand with occasionally a little grouping of artificial trees. Bonseki is the art of arranging black stones and white sand on a serenely lustrous black lacquer tray of approximately the same measurements as bonkei. The landscapes suggest distant scenes of mountain, river, lake or sea and shoreline.

It is remarkable how many moods of scenery and weather can thus be pictured—a rising sun, a full moon, storm or fine weather, calm sea or angry waves dashing against rocks, a little pond in spring break-up, a tumbling waterfall, all with just a few rocks and a few spoonfuls of different grades of white sand. A modern bonseki has even been made of these materials with Niagara Falls as inspiration.

In bonseki, mountains and hills are suggested by white sand cleverly spread almost flat on a black tray to create distant heights. Rocks, usually black, are then placed to form islands or rocky promontories of the shoreline. These rocks will have been eagerly collected, scrubbed with a stiff brush to clean them and then sawed to give a flat surface so that they will sit level. They will be used over and over again in many different scenes. White sand is used with great artistry to create the illusion of breaking waves, tumbling rivers, mountain peaks or floating clouds. Finishing touches to the surface of the sand are made with feathers, cut and trimmed especially for this purpose.

For years the aristocracy in Japan were the main devotees of the art of bonseki, but today people of all classes are becoming eager students. Three schools, Hosokawa, Yenzan and Ishikawa, offer a diploma course which takes five years to complete. The bonseki made for us by Mrs. Baika Yashiro of the Hosokawa School, are titled *Low Tide at Sugita* and *A Scene at Miho-no-Matsubara*, one of the famous scenic spots of Japan (Illustrations 40 and 41).

We know of no effort to apply the art of bonseki to America. Should such a movement start, there is certainly no lack of inspiration in the moody shorelines of our coasts and great inland lakes. Our majestic mountains both west and east could surely be as inspiring as Mount Fujiyama.

For visitors to Japan who might wish to see a display of bonseki

(40)

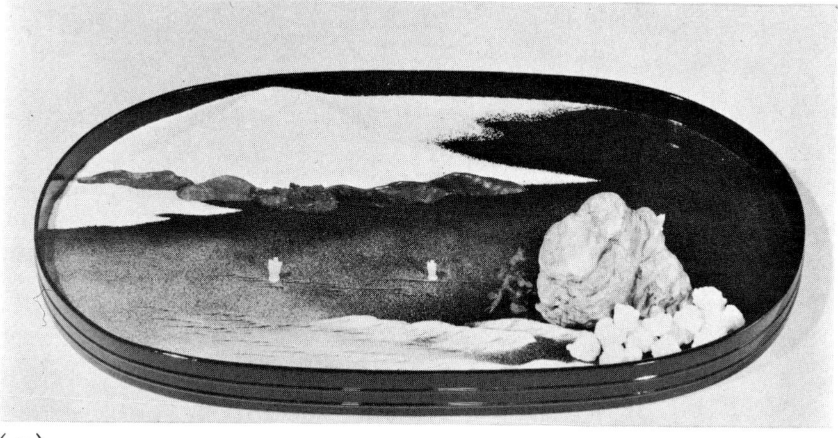

(41)

ILLUSTRATIONS 40, 41. BONSEKI

Tray landscapes, representing two famous scenes in Japan. 40. *Low Tide at Sugita.* 41. *Miho-no-Matsubara,* a favorite place with artists. Both by Mrs. Baika Yashiro of the Hosokawa School in Tokyo.

or bonkei, a tour of a school can usually be arranged where master and students can be seen at work. Exhibitions are also often held in the large department stores in Japan. For reading, we warmly recommend *Tray Landscapes,* published by the Japan Travel Bureau in Tokyo, a well-compiled and inexpensive little book.

Thus we find the stream of miniature art flowing steadily and strongly from earliest times into today. We are shown, first hand, that it existed, in the artifacts of museum collections all over the land. We are even able to buy reproductions of some of the best of them as inspiration for our own work. Still others we may see in photographs or read about as we pursue this fascinating art. In the bonsai, mame bonsai, bonkei and bonseki of Japan, we find a sympathetic appreciation, going back hundreds of years, of the miniature possibilities in growing plants. The maker of miniatures today who seeks out these examples in history will surely be stimulated by them.

PART TWO

Miniature Arrangements with Flowers

3.

The Wide World of Miniatures

THE most exciting thing that happens to an arranger of miniature flowers is that Nature's world suddenly has a new dimension. Bud, twig, tendril, flower, leaf and seed all have new through-the-looking-glass beauty that gives endless pleasure in its discovery, endless joy in its use, endless spark to the imagination.

The skilful use of this material is what we see in a finished arrangement in a flower show, a photograph, in a book, or perhaps as a decoration in someone's house. But this is only the finale to what has been a delightful experience right from the beginning. Experienced miniature arrangers as often as novices get a thrill out of gathering their props and materials. Random it nearly always is, full of surprises also but dull never.

CLOSE AT HAND

On a walk in familiar woods searching for miniature things, you will find beauty you never knew was there—the breaking bud on a shoot of elder, green long before there is any other sign of life in the spring, a burst of white parachute fungi less than a quarter of an inch across, spurting on black wire stems from a peaty stump on a moist summer day, the prickly hat from a beechnut discarded by a hungry chipmunk filling his storehouse in the fall. All these things are suddenly interesting to you not just for themselves but because you are going to use them yourself to create something lovely.

Each time of year will bring different plants before this new vision of yours. Unseasonable weather will often produce materials which you may never have seen before, though you have been making miniatures for years. Such was the summer just gone, when warm, moist cloudy weather went on for weeks and weeks, and strange mosses, lichens, toadstools and mushrooms I had never seen in forty years of plant hunting pushed their way into the world from grass and leaf mold and rotting stump.

Sometimes a strange combination of weather—and perhaps bees—will dazzle the mountain ash trees or the milkweeds into great crops of orange berries or silky seeds, or the tiny plants at the swamp's edge, gold threads and pipsissewas, will have more lustrous crops than you can ever remember before.

With these beguiling strangers, your arrangements will be particularly inspired, for as you make them you will combine skill with wonder. Book rules will fly out the window, clumsy fingers will become deft, for the beauty of the little plant itself will be your teacher.

Unlikely places, boulevards and ditches, railway banks and vacant lots, can provide new plants for your list. There is a construction company yard for storing bulldozers about a mile from our house that I always explore every September to find new things for my collection. This year it was about a dozen little seedling dandelion plants from one to two inches in diameter growing flat against the hard clay. I dug them out carefully, carried them home in a piece of tissue and pressed them between weighted papers. At Christmastime I used them as snowflakes and stars in a silhouette landscape for a window pane. My favorite wild flowers are always growing there too. Frothy white Queen Anne's lace and golden buttercups, miniscule yellow clovers and tangled on the fence the curved-back turks caps of purple nightshade with their yellow drops. All have a special beauty and usefulness in small bouquets.

For outline and vertical emphasis, there is nothing so good as some of the sedges and grasses of the fields and wet places. These are

(42) *Lockwood Haight*

ILLUSTRATION 42. FRAGMENTS OF SPRINGTIME

Treasures of the spring garden, spiraea, lily-of-the-valley, forget-me-not, ivy, perennial daisy, viburnum and creeping Jenny look charming in small pottery containers. Average height four inches. Arranged by Helen Murray.

plants not known to many and often overlooked, yet their variety is amazing and almost all are unusual and suggest countless new designs, both fresh and dried. Some have wispy twists of leaf, some bold lances. Seeds of some are prickly dark brown balls held in clusters. Others are dripping curves of beigey pearls.

LET YOUR GARDEN BE A STOREHOUSE

Once interested in miniatures, you will find yourself choosing new plants for your garden with a more critical eye and a new standard. You will want new varieties that produce small-scale material like sweet autumn clematis, *Clematis paniculata*, a vine with showers of pale green, late summer stars. Any or all of the heathers—pink, red and white provide both flowers and foliage for many months of the year. You will find a few plants of the chunky *Juniper blauuwi* invaluable for conical evergreen shapes, no longer than your thumb, and all the boxwoods wonderfully handy for long-lasting shiny green foliage.

Almost every rock-garden plant has flowers or leaves, sometimes both, that are the right scale for miniatures. The white, pink and purple stars of perennial *Phlox subulata*, crisp white arabis and candytuft all flower in early spring. The various creeping thymes and the six-inch, rose-spired *Veronica rosea* bloom nearly all summer, and the glossy leaves of the thymes being pungently fragrant are a special dividend for a sick-room miniature arrangement. Growers in different parts of the country supply these rock garden plants in varieties that are hardy for their area. You would be wise to check with them before you buy.

Although most annuals are properly big and showy, there are a number that produce small flowers or florets. All the alyssums are marvellous, for their blooming time stretches from early spring to stiff hard frost in fall. Lobelia, harder to grow but the most intense deep blue, is a delicate little flower—comes in pale blue and white too. Ageratum and mignonette are two fluff accents, one lavender blue, one a strange yellow-green with bits of orange. There are even minute zinnias (Red Riding Hood) and marigolds (Gnome) that you may never have seen. Verbena, both fragile and fragrant, I can never resist using, although it shatters easily. But the colors are so lucent!

(43) Roche

ILLUSTRATION 43. THE LITTLEST DAFFODIL

Narcissus minimus, barely an inch long and certainly the sweetest miniature bulb of the spring garden, with a few catkins in a simple brown bowl. Arranged by Mary Alice Roche.

Once you develop an enthusiasm for miniatures, you will be sending to far-away places for seeds. Last year, in a new catalogue, I found a violetta only half an inch across and with the perfume of wild violets. Developed by Howard Crane of England, it has turned out to be a pet, constantly in bloom, really fragrant and some of the plants even winter hardy in our garden in Canada. To make miniature flower arrangements with such material, picked when you want it because it is there in your own garden, is indeed a joy.

Nor should you overlook herbs and vegetables, whether you grow them yourself or buy them. Dill makes the frilliest of bright yellow accents in a flowery bouquet, and lavender is a dainty vertical, —scented too. Parsley is a pert green for foliage and the blades of chives make a bold line. There is even a tomato (Tiny Tim) with fragile yellow flowers less than half an inch long and little green fruits to match (Color Plate 7).

Fruit and vegetable arrangements are easy to make with cranberries, wild strawberries, brussels sprouts, cauliflower florets, broccoli, peas and the ferny tops of carrots. And do not overlook the dainty flowers of potatoes. It is said that Queen Victoria thought these so beautiful she often pinned them in her hair!

FROM YOUR FLORIST

With the quick flights of flowers by plane from all over the world, your florist's shop is added to the list of places to look for miniature material. Many imported varieties will be fresh in form, some even exotic, and therefore fun to work with. In Toronto, where I live, we have at least one planeload of flowers coming in each week during the winter from the sunny fields of California, others from Florida, Mexico, Hawaii and occasionally from Italy. Thus we have the fluffy yellow flower balls and gray ferny foliage of acacia, the miniature snapdragon shapes and colors of linaria, gorgeous cerise heather all winter, wax flower with the Victorian puce blossom and needle foliage smelling like lemon verbena when it is pinched, and a spray-branch euphorbia with brilliant orange clusters of quarter-inch flowers. As the market grows, even more varieties will be added to the list.

PLATE I. GARDEN BY A POOL. A weeping potentilla tree, barely three inches high, bends over a blue pool with agate islands. The yellow lilies are made of stonecrop florets, the evergreen tree from a one-inch tip of *Juniper chinensis blauuwi*. Overall height four inches. Arrangement by the author.

PLATE 2. A MINIATURE MERRY CHRISTMAS. Two golden Mexican angels hold aloft flowery sconces of grasses, berries and immortelles; in the center stands a little boxwood tree wound round with garlands of multiflora rose hips; a tiny white angel stands guard over all. The tree stands on a wet oasis base in a brass, footed saucer. Height less than six inches. Arrangement by Barbara Ann Hynes.

(3)

(4)

(5)

(6)

Plates 3-6. Bonsai and Bonkei. 3 and 4. Mame or baby bonsai, a few inches high and some of them twenty years old, one with a tiny perfect quince, are from the collection of Zeko Nakamura. 5. A Peaceful Garden, a Japanese bonkei or tray landscape. 6. One of the Eight Beauty Spots Around Lake Biwa. Mountain and rocks in this bonkei are of *keto* peat, which can be modeled and painted to look like stone. Trees are true dwarfs. Both by Koshyu Oyama; all photographs by Nihon Hasshoku.

PLATES 7-10. RARE AND EVERYDAY CONTAINERS. 7. An herb arrangement with chives, mint, Tiny Tim tomato flowers and a little tomato for accessory in a vanilla bottle top on a button. Less than five inches high. Arrangement by author. 8. An exquisite Chinese lady in coral beside a twist of ivy and a cluster of spice bush on mutton fat jade with its own carved stand. Less than four inches high. Arrangement by Helen Murray. 9. In antique miniature silver containers on raised jewellers' velvet blocks: a French basket with May flowers and grass; Adam-style open salt with spiraea and ferns; sterling bowl with foam flower, deutzia, forget-me-nots and maiden pinks *(Dianthus deltoides)* with a frosted crystal Venus as accessory. All heights two and three inches. 10. A bold-line arrangement of manzanita twigs, juniper and double rose begonia. Height three inches. Both arranged by Barbara Ann Hynes.

MINIATURE MAKINGS FROM FAR AWAY

Finding unexpected treasure among plants of your woods and gardens at home is nothing to the excitement of hunting miniature makings when you travel. An interest in dried materials particularly will make you an avid explorer, and with this type you will not have to worry about regulations for plant importation as you would if you wished to bring back living plants.

Some of my real prizes have been casuarina cones from the Bahamas, each less than an inch long, but most tidily cast and with an ideal still-life look. I brought home a dozen in the toe of a shoe in my suitcase. Bunches of rosy red pepper berries from California I once tucked in a piece of tissue in my purse; I gathered bright scarlet holly berries and tamarack cones in the northwoods of Ontario and green sycamore balls in Virginia. And in Florida I picked up little buttons of palm seeds and strings of white seaweed that looked for all the world like crocheted white lace—ideal for shell arrangements.

I should warn you that this kind of dedication may make you rather lonely at first. Children and husband tend to walk away quickly pretending they do not know you as you scramble around looking for little things. But persevere, for in time they accept you as a lovable eccentric to be humored and you will find all kinds of strange offerings presented for your grace and favor. My small daughter, a budding miniaturist if ever I saw one, has the most fantastic eye for "liney" things. She often brings me a grape vine tendril twisting back and forth in perfect balance, or a piece of wild milkweed vine, each pod poised at just the right angle on its winding stem and the seeds breaking out in just the right places.

CREATION OF BEAUTY FROM THE COMMONPLACE

Having taught yourself to look for miniature beauty, having gathered it in, you then learn to enhance it by arranging it well. You may use a flower or plant alone, or you may set it with others for contrast or harmony in a container that makes it a picture wherever it is. I remember the first miniature flower arrangement I ever made. It was a wild white violet (Viola odorata pallens), the smallest of the species. I had found it blooming very early in spring on a mossy little island in a woodland pool. Its haunting fragrance, the minute purple veining of its throat, the proud way it held its head high on the fragile stem all entranced me. I wet my handkerchief in the ice-cold water of the pool and wrapped violet and leaves in it to carry them home. I found a delicate porcelain Chinese inkwell, made a holder of wire and clay and put the little violet in it off to one side and with an expanse of water showing, as it had been in the woods. I had such pleasure glancing at it as long as it lived that I have never stopped making miniatures since.

Spring is of course a marvellous time for miniature-making, for material is at every hand, but other seasons offer opportunities too. You may find yourself, as I did once, planning a visit to a gardening friend so ill that most bouquets had to be banned from her room. From my summer garden, I picked her a tiny bunch of fragrant flowers—verbena, lavender, heliotrope, the littlest marigold you ever saw, only as big as a thumb nail, and polished green thyme for foliage. I arranged them firmly in a block of wet oasis on a footed white porcelain cup so that they might stay fresh for many days within glancing distance of her pillow. She has told me since that that bouquet was one of the great pleasures of her life.

Autumn has its own small-world bounty—everlastings, berries and seed pods gay and bright when fresh, and wonderful dried for winter bouquets. Bright orange berries of bittersweet, *Celastrus loeseneri* of our gardens and *C. scandens* of the woods, offer clean-cut shapes and bright color, and go especially well with driftwood bits or the soft gray of wild sage or sea lavender. Inch-long bunches of black privet berries store well for times when you want grape-shaped clusters for a plenteous arrangement in a little marble urn. Buds, picked from sideshoots of strawflowers, yield bright everlastings like little roses, and you will store and keep them carefully, for they have a thousand uses.

When winter robs the world of tender things, there are still clever arrangements to be made with twigs, bits of dried grasses that you may find sticking through the snow, and all the forms of evergreens. Many plants—small ivies, shoots of *Euonymous kewensis* (a most useful little plant), the shining leaves of gold thread and wintergreen, the tree form of club moss—will take up glycerine well

(44) *Roche*

ILLUSTRATION 44. SNOWDROPS

Half a dozen snowdrops plucked from the cold, late winter ground to remind the household that spring is really on the way. Height five inches. Arranged by Mary Alice Roche.

and thus be preserved for a long, long time. Some of them will even take on a fresh green color, rather than the usual bronze of glycerined leaves, if you mix a little green and yellow food coloring with the solution. I use a mixture of one-third glycerine and two-thirds warm water with a few drops of food coloring. The smallest leaves are immersed in the solution. With the larger ones, I stand the lower third of the stem in the mixture and watch for it to appear up in the leaves. In about three weeks, it is fully absorbed and then you have a supply of lovely foliage that will last for years. Of course, plants under conservation protection should be gathered only if you grow them yourself.

4.

Design and Containers

THE increasing interest in miniatures, which we see on every hand today, appears at a time when flower arranging as an art in America has come of age. We are beyond the period of early learning. We are beyond the time when arrangers adhered to rigid rules which often produced contrived compositions that repulsed rather than attracted. Our best arrangers today, and there are thousands of them all over our country, eagerly create designs that spring spontaneously from joy in artistic expression, more often than not the natural beauty of the flower itself suggesting the design. They know that to enhance this natural beauty to its fullest they must still respect basic principles and work hard to apply them well.

They accept that pleasing balance follows careful placement. They use flowing line and thoughtful repetition to give rhythmic beauty. They appreciate the need for variety yet with harmony in form and shape. They are familiar with the mathematics of proportion and scale not only within the outline of the arrangement but in the relation of that arrangement to its surroundings. They have given new thought in the last few years to implying a dimension of depth. They have succeeded in opening up their designs with a sense of airiness they did not have before. They use patterns of flower heads, stems and seed capsules with ease.

And like all artists whose skill is maturing, they have learned their lessons so well that now they know how and when to break the rules artistically. As Helen Van Pelt Wilson has said so aptly in *The Joy of Flower Arranging* (Barrows), "I think that as experts progress, like all who are accomplished, they forget how much they know; actually they instinctively follow those rules which have been evolved from principles of design and which they have, as rules, forgotten."

With this experience and new freedom, arrangers now turn to miniatures as a stimulating challenge to their skill. Successful work in this medium, they find, calls for exciting new talent, new ability. Restraint becomes more important than in large-scale pieces, for there is not space to be diffuse. Simplicity is essential. Each twig, each flower must be arranged to add tellingly to the whole effect, if the final design is to be good.

Material is bountiful and the best of it wild. Suddenly a whole new world opens, the world of nature's most fascinating small things. This in itself is stimulating, for if you scratch the surface of a flower arranger a botanist often shows through.

Containers, always important to the whole design, can be collector's pieces or ingenious understudies, and the hunt for just the right one can lead through the trays of a button department or into an antique store specializing in crystal salt cellars. Your purse need not be fat, nor your shelves too capacious for any of them.

Eventually there is for both material and container the discipline of measure, of accepted flower-show rules for what may be the size of a miniature, and this, to flower arrangers, is the most stirring challenge of all.

THE MEASURE OF A MINIATURE

The most widely accepted measure for a miniature is that of the National Council of State Garden Clubs of the United States, which calls for the height or width to be not over five inches. The National Association of Flower Arrangement Societies of Great Britain sets their measurement at four inches, and flower arrangers and bonsai-

(45) *Lockwood Haight*

ILLUSTRATION 45. GUIDE TO MEASUREMENT

For your own pleasure, miniatures are in scale if they are not taller or wider than the span of your hand; for competition and official shows the accepted measurement is five inches. This one is life size, of variegated ivy with scarlet crown-of-thorn flowers in a pewter vase on a piece of gray, green, and white slag glass. Arranged by the author.

makers in Japan use two inches and under for miniature classes, five inches and under for "small" arrangements.

We all accept these rulings when miniatures are to be exhibited in competitive classes and judged. If however, your own pleasure is the only measure and your own house or a gift is its use, I consider that a flower arrangement is miniature if it is as tall or as wide as the span of your hand from the tip of your thumb to the apex of your forefinger. This, for most people, is five to seven inches, but the best point of such a measure is that it is individually scaled to you. I think that this is a far better way to decide what is "miniature," unless the arrangement must be judged; in this case, of course, show rulings must be followed.

FOR NOVICE ARRANGERS

Although most arrangers first learn the skill of making large compositions and then apply their knowledge to miniatures, there is no reason why the novice should not work right from the start in the small size. The same formula of study, practice, analysis and more practice will bring success both in home arrangements and in shows. In the beginning, it will be useful to study a good text on general design in flower arranging and apply its points, one by one, to miniature-making. We recommend two such books: *Design for Flower Arrangers* by Dorothy W. Reister (Van Nostrand), and *Design in Flower Arrangement* by John Taylor and Dorothy Noyes Arms (Macmillan).

IMPORTANCE OF SCALE

When you apply the principles of design to miniatures, scale is the most stirring challenge of all. With something so small it is important that every part should harmonize. One flower too large and the whole loses essential quality. A container or an accessory not small enough dooms the finished picture right at the start.

In a five-inch arrangement, for instance, the container may rarely exceed two inches in height or width without being out of scale. It may be a shade taller if a cascading arrangement is used. It may be a little wider if the whole design of the arrangement is within the container as it might be in a water scene of a little planting. Similarly, plant material should usually extend no more than three inches up from the rim of the container for a vertical arrangement nor spread wider than a total of three inches across, for a horizontal one.

A COMMON FAULT

By far the most common fault of both experienced and novice arrangers is the use of flowers too big for the total scale. Most choose twigs, berries and leaves in appropriate sizes but go astray in their choice of flowers. I have seen countless exhibitors, fascinated by the little *minimus* daffodil, which has a trumpet about an inch long, use it in a five-inch arrangement. I have yet to see it used in appropriate scale. It is always too big.

Although some exhibitors think that judges are splitting hairs when they do not allow de-petalling a large flower to make it smaller, nor trimming a flower to reduce its size, most arrangers agree with such rulings and find plenty to inspire them in more natural things.

MINIATURE FLOWER ARRANGEMENTS IN JAPAN TODAY

Japanese arrangers, who have been practicing their art far longer than we in the West, are moving into the field of abstract design in much of their work. Miss Kasumi Teshigawara, daughter of Sofu Teshigarawa, founder of the famous Sogetsu School of Flower Arrangement in Japan, is recognized as one of the most talented arrangers working in this new style. Her favorite designs are abstract and although arrangers accustomed to classical Japanese styles may at first glance find them strange, close study will show them to be both fanciful and fresh.

Seeming at first to abandon the familiar precepts of traditional Japanese flower arrangement, the design reveals, under careful examination, that it still follows the basic principles that have attracted so many to Japanese styles in the past. Miss Teshigawara, who has made a set of miniatures for us to illustrate this new thought, uses for the most part containers of pottery in plain shapes, each only a little over an inch high. Her plant material is the familiar chrysanthemum, bamboo and peach and she still prunes out line for rhythm and carries a flower back for the traditional look-through view. But she uses bold accents; in the case of this set, she twists gold-colored wire as an auxiliary to the main design, and the often severe pattern that these lines create adds a new and dominating element to the design.

Miss Teshigawara's arrangements are, as their traditional forbears were, fascinating as an expression of a people for whom flower arrangement is a respected and beloved ceremony of the common day.

(46)

ILLUSTRATION 46. KASUMI TESHIGAWARA

Leading miniature flower arranger of Japan, daughter of Sogetsu Teshigawara, founder of the Sogetsu School in Tokyo, creates in her studio new, abstract designs, with traditional materials.

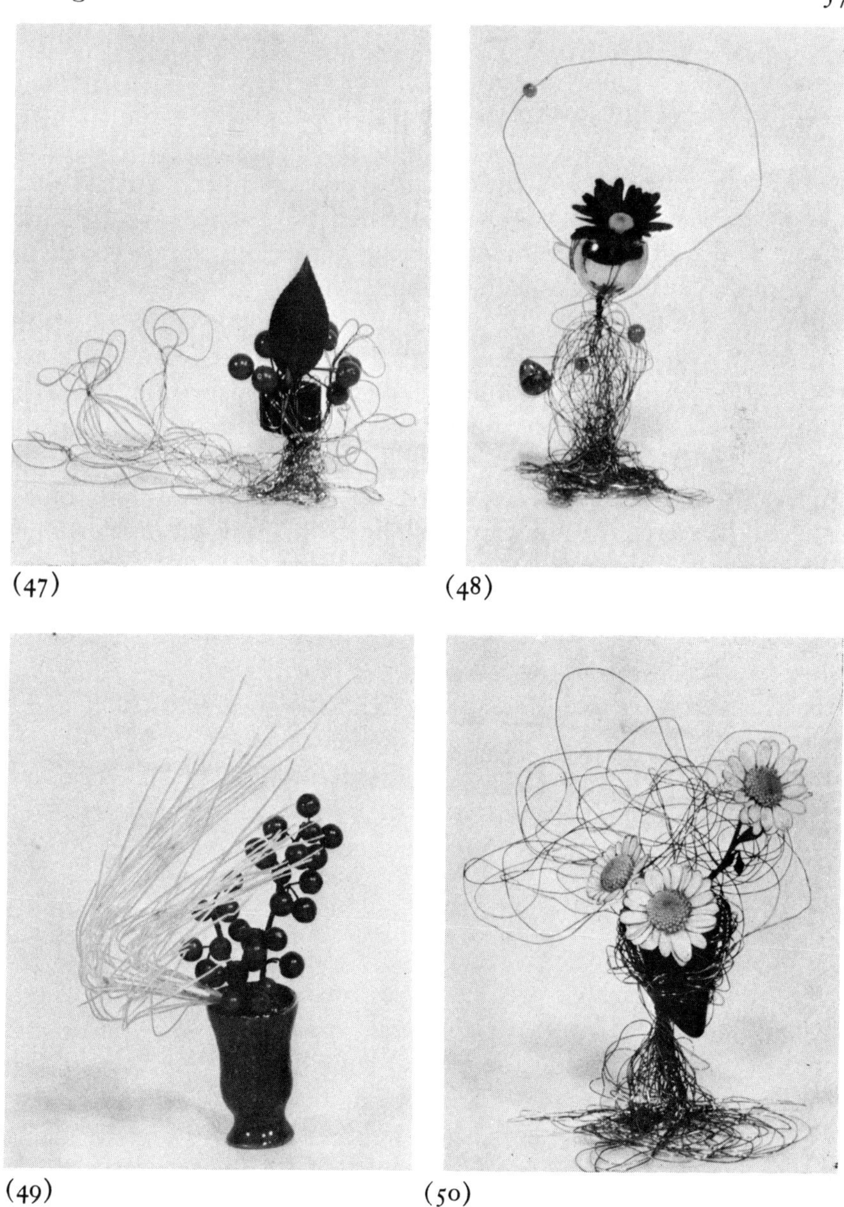

(47) (48)

(49) (50)

ILLUSTRATIONS 47–50. JAPANESE ABSTRACT MINIATURE ARRANGEMENTS

Traditional plant materials—peach, camellia, bamboo, chrysanthemum, azalea and rose—are used here by Kasumi Teshigawara in untraditional designs of bold line and with such accessories as twisted gold wire. Containers are mainly of pottery, occasionally a bottle top.

FASCINATION OF MINIATURE CONTAINERS

Almost any small shape that will hold water can become a container for a fresh-flower miniature. Almost any small shape, whether it will hold water or not, can become a container for a dried flower miniature. You can spin a charming web for memory with a tiny design of flower and leaves in something as precious as a carved piece of antique jade, or as ingenious as a smooth, plastic button, or as natural as the textured boat of milkweed pod. For a rooted plant, perhaps a two-inch pine already gnarled at three years old, your container can be an especially-made Japanese pot complete with drainage hole. For a bizarre and bold succulent, a severe block of plain pottery is suitable to set off the weird form.

Collecting containers can be a hobby in itself. I can think of no limit to the search for miniature containers, nor any greater fun than when you find a particularly good one. Cosmetic counters, antique shops, hardware stores, toy counters, sea shores, woods and lakes, button departments, gift shops, handcraft centers, museums and galleries, all are favored ground for the hunter. Even the bottle of vanilla on your kitchen shelf yields a top that will pass for an ebony pot, the perfect container for an elf-sized bouquet of herbs, perhaps chives, Tiny Tim tomatoes and shoots of garden mint with an accessory green tomato no more than a quarter-inch in diameter.

OF SILVER AND COPPER

Except by happy accident, you are not likely to be able to acquire any large number of miniature containers or accessories in one place. Your most cherished pieces will be picked up here and there, one at a time, not because you are searching for them but because you are always alert to the possibilities of finding good ones. The sterling silver open salt, made more than a hundred years ago in the melon shape of a soup tureen and filled with a bright winter bouquet of heather in the wall set in Illustration 74 was picked up in a hotel gift shop in Victoria, B.C., overlooking the wide Pacific. The graceful pedestal silver salt cellar in Color Plate 14 shows all the daintiness of traditional Florentine work; it was bought on the *Christophoro Columbo* as she sailed the blue Mediterranean between Gibraltar and

Naples. Then there is the two-inch saucer, deep blue enamel on copper, which holds the fairy lake scene of a little tree, floating flowers and agate islands (and this is, I think, my favorite miniature). It was bought in a small handcraft shop a few blocks from my home (Color Plate 1).

Many exquisite containers are imported, as they have been for many years, from that seemingly inexhaustible storehouse of lovely things, Japan and the Far East port of Hong Kong. Never pass a store showing oriental objects without going in to look around, for you never know what treasures you may find.

Fourteen three-inch pewter-washed copper vases and bowls beautifully made with intricate, fitted tops were bought in such a shop for fifty cents apiece. Although the owner wailed, "Madam, you are buying my entire stock," I am glad I did, for they are among my most cherished treasures with a natural harmony when used as a set.

IN PORCELAIN, JADE AND CRYSTAL

More fragile, but equally well-proportioned, are the pale porcelains that you often find in Japanese shops. Sometimes they have a bold or a faint pattern, sometimes a matching top, nearly always they have a tiny, carved, and well-scaled stand to set them off. A pair of these, bluish white and less than three inches high, with arrangements of drippy, species pink begonias and waxy leaves took first prize in a miniature class I judged a few years ago. They had been bought in the Chinese section of Victoria, B.C., for less than a dollar each including the stands, which were only an inch in diameter.

Dark green soapstone and mutton fat jade, although not cheap, are usually available through regular import outlets. They are treasures for the years, either with flowers in them or as ornaments on your shelves with other miniatures. The most beautiful of these that I have ever seen was a rectangular suiban in the creamy luster of mutton fat jade. It came with a shipment of ivories, jades and corals from Japan. Carved on one corner with a delicate lotus flower and leaf, it stood on its own rubbed teakwood stand. Its christening flowers were an arrangement of clematis tendril, ferns, and flowers of the baby bluebell, *Campanula muralis.* To find a container of such beauty makes you tingle all over not only when you look at it, but when you think about it too.

(51) *Lockwood Haight*

ILLUSTRATION 51. GOOD CONTAINERS

Almost anything makes a good container for miniatures. On the left at the back are shown small pottery shapes, some designed for mame bonsai trees; at the left front, a group of buttons; center rear, a pewter plate, stone, and vase; in the center, a silver perfume bottle and vases; center front, light sockets, bottle top, driftwood and brass pipes; center right and far right, cups and saucers, a pitcher, a pepper shaker, flat plates and liqueur bowl; right rear, three open salts, two silver and one crystal; on top of the block, two sake cups, one footed, a vase with lid and stand, a marble urn, and a carved ivory vase with a false bottom used to smuggle drugs. The measure on the block is in inches. Author's collection.

If you find the hunt for true miniature containers a delight, it is nothing to the pleasure you will know when you find something designed for another use, but adaptable for flowers. In fine materials, there are exquisite small open salt cellars in modern silver and glass. Only a few weeks ago, I found a David Andersen sterling open salt in the shape of a Norwegian Viking ship, with a liner of royal blue glass. In the same shop, there was also a small, open mustard bowl of rubbed maple wood, just an inch high and barely two wide. This had been made in Quebec. Both of these I coated with paraffin wax before the pinholder was fixed into them, so that water and clay would not stain them. This is a good plan to follow with all fine pieces.

From Denmark come enameled porcelain liqueur cups as thin as eggshells that make lovely containers, as you will see in the brown cup with casuarina cones in a wall setting (Illustration 76); and from Sweden come pedestal crystal liqueur glasses as clear and thin as bubbles that are great favorites with arrangers of traditional bouquets.

NEW ANGLE FOR ANTIQUING

If old rather than contemporary things please you, then search in antique shops. Once you begin to be aware of possibilities, only your purse and your stamina will limit you. An antique silver perfume bottle, an inch and a quarter high, could have a single tiny rose. A filigree silver nut basket will hold a cluster of Paul's Scarlet thorn blossom that could pass for heavy headed peonies seen through a wrong-way spy glass. (Color Plate 16). Inkwells, salt shakers, little lamps, snuff and pill boxes—a thousand things, will round out your collection and at no great expense, with no great storage problem and no heavy parcel to carry home.

FROM YOUR DRESSING TABLE

Perfume bottles, lipstick cases, lids of cosmetic jars, little boxes for bobby pins, pill bottles, pocket mirrors—your ingenious eye will never stop searching. One of my favorites in this class was a ribbon winner in a flower show a few years ago. A shallow plastic box, once used for hairpins, was painted dull black. In it, on a low pedestal made from a plastic dental floss bottle, also painted black, was a tiny piece of what looked like abstract green glass sculpture. At the base, planted

(52) *Lockwood Haight*

ILLUSTRATION 52. IN ODD CONTAINERS

A champagne cork (above), shells and coral (below left), the base of a Chinese inkwell (center) and a driftwood chip (below right) make excellent containers for bits of dried flowers—goldenrod, strawflower, globe amaranth, meadowsweet and fern, grape tendrils, fungi and the glycerinized leaves of gold thread. Arranged by Margaret Farwell. Average height three inches.

in white sand, were the minutest of white violets with green lily-of-the-valley buds behind for high line and green ivy for low. The sculpture was a piece of glass that had melted in the heat of a burned house and had been found in the ashes!

Another little beauty was a graceful chalice, no more than two and a half inches high, done with grape tendril, cotoneaster leaves and raspberry red epimediums—a perfect flower for miniatures. It had been, to begin with, a container for colored sugar pellets from a candy counter. Painted black and glued to a small black stand—so that it would not tip over—and adorned with this sensitively handled arrangement, it easily won Best-in-Show for the day.

RÔLE OF THE BUTTON

A very special source, almost as limitless as seashells, is buttons. They are particularly good for dried arrangements, but there are also some with little hollows deep enough to hold a damp piece of oasis for fresh flowers, if you first plug the sewing holes with clay. (Color Plate 16). After a few months of collecting miniature containers, you will be so used to looking for good ones you will never walk past a button counter without stopping to size up possibilities. Sales clerks will think you daft, but fortunately buttons are usually fully displayed and you can, without going into harrowing detail, ask for one of these and one of those, and then make a quick getaway. And all for only a few cents.

AT THE STORE AND IN THE FIELDS

The hardware store will offer a new adventure. You go in to get light bulbs, have the iron fixed, pick up a little paint and what do you come out with? Rubber ends for canes, plastic tips for furniture, the bottom of a brass light socket, a few squares of thin copper to hammer out shallow trays, some small pieces of lead to bend into little bowls, a dozen bits of mirror only a few inches square to make small dried arrangements for a party (Illustration 53).

Then start out through the garden, the woods, the seashore. Bits of weathered wood, poppy-seed heads cut cleanly off and turned upside down, clam and oyster shells, angelswing shells, milkweed pods, there will seem to be no end to the shapes and forms that trip

(53) *Lockwood Haight*

ILLUSTRATION 53. BRASS SOCKET AND OTHER CONTAINERS
The base of brass light sockets (center), a bit of wooden dowel (left center), a button (left) and a set of small brass tubes (right) with cedar cones, hardhack, fern, dock, pine needles, pearly everlasting, bittersweet and pepper berries. Average height, three inches. Arranged by Margaret Farwell.

the quick levers of your brain into action and your gathering fingers to picking them up and bringing them home. Here you have the makings of thousands of happy memories as well as clever miniatures.

AS GIFTS

Your newly alert eye is bound to be noticed by others. Friends and family in no time at all will begin to bring you treasures they have found to add to your collection of containers and tiny figures. The miniature-maker is as much a boon to a small son with only a week's allowance to spend on Mother's birthday present as to the air-traveling friend with only ounces to spare in his baggage for gifts to bring home. Fate may even play into your miniature collection as it did into mine when a thoughtful friend, traveling in Greece, bought for me a two-inch reproduction of an authentic ancient vase. Worried that it might get lost in the welter of tissue paper wrapped around larger presents in her suitcase, she wound a piece of cotton wool around the little vase and carefully tucked it into her purse. The suitcase of big presents was lost somewhere en route and the only memento anybody got, including my friend herself, was the little vase she brought for me.

Having such presents from far away places is fun in your own house, but it is nothing compared to the pleasure of using them in a scheduled miniature class in a flower show. Competing with other arrangers is one of the chief joys of miniature flower arranging. And the laurels—is there a miniature laurel?—usually go to the arranger with ingenuity, imagination and that vitally important, alert eye of the observant collector.

5.

Accessories in Scale

THE making of miniature sculptures, carvings and other ornament is old as an art. The possibilities therefore of finding good accessories carved, molded or shaped by any means in any one of a thousand woods, stones, metals or materials are almost limitless, for such things have been made for hundreds of years and are still being made universally to-day.

We turn again first, as we do for the finest and best designed containers, to the East or sources importing from the East. Here we find tiny figures, animals, miniature cottages and bridges, gates, birds, fish, all in the finest detail and sometimes in materials as lasting as bronze. What could be more exquisite than the elegant coral lady or the little figure beside the rose begonias in Color Plates 8 and 10.

FROM TOY STORES

Here we find adorable things, frisky little lambs, rabbits, toads, turtles, dolls, all sorts of things, often beautifully made and sometimes in unbreakable plastic. These are the furnishings of the child's world of make-believe, but they are in fine scale for flower arrangements.

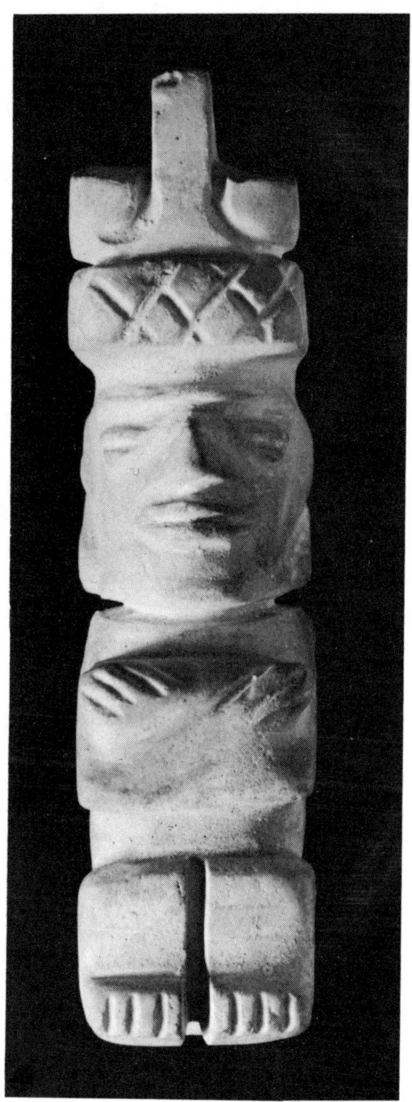

(56)

(54) *Top* (55) *Lower*

ILLUSTRATIONS 54–56. MUSEUM REPRODUCTIONS AS ACCESSORIES

No more than a few inches high, and reproduced in either a synthetic stone or metal, these represent widely divergent cultures. 54. Ornament from Panama, original in the Cleveland Museum of Art, Cleveland, Ohio. 55. Rooster from Syria, original in Dumbarton Oaks Research Library, Washington, D.C. 56. Mexican Man with Fancy Headdress, original in Smithsonian Institution, Washington, D.C. All reproductions by Alva Museum Replicas, Inc., New York.

FROM NATURE

We turn also to nature's vast storehouse to find pebbles, shells, fungi, stones, wood, even weeds. To make a pretty base and disguise a pinholder use a bit of woolly gray lichen in a white violet arrangement (Color Plate 28). Much of the charm of miniatures lies in the fact that this fragment of loveliness which is normally swallowed up in the immense beauty of the earth, is here lifted out of its complicated natural setting and, combined with material that harmonizes and also enhances it, is simplified and set out for us to enjoy.

STANDS AND BASES

Nothing so sets off a good show piece as a well-chosen base. And at home a base also often saves a fine table or desk from errant drip.

Buttons are constantly useful, especially flat, black plastic ones in different sizes. You will notice that they have often been used in our illustrations. Jar tops, slices of natural wood, carved stands from jewelry as well as antique shops—you can never have too many both in size and material. Occasionally you will want something exactly in the spirit of the arrangement you are making, like a little lace doily I have used under a silver boat with roses. It is actually a plastic Italian copy of real Point de Venise lace and cost the staggering sum of ten cents.

The ingenious son of one miniature arranger made a Christmas present for her of twenty little black scroll stands from old phonograph records. He warmed the records in the oven until they were pliable, then cut and shaped them to different sizes. They made such a hit that he not only pleased his mother but earned all his pocket money for the rest of the year filling orders for her friends.

THE DETERMINING ACCESSORY

As you travel about the world, collecting here and there some treasured bit, you will find small figures among modern ornament that you will particularly enjoy having in your collection. Such, for instance, is the pair of nuns from Italy making a joyful noise unto the Lord in the most fragile ceramic, as we use them in Illustration 75, the ivory Eskimo puffin backed by a drift of flowers in Color Plate 21 and the ethereal and frosty crystal Venus in the little grouping in Color Plate 9. The gray velvet blocks, supporting the arrangements in this picture, are actually stands for a jeweler's window. These ornaments are a pleasure to have but they look twice as lovely, if you make a setting of miniature flowers for them.

6.

More Flowers and Plants for Miniatures

"WHERE on earth do you find such tiny flowers and leaves for your miniatures?" I am often asked. Truthfully I answer, "The world is overflowing with them." Every square foot of garden, every leafy patch of woodland, every bench in a greenhouse of mixed plants, all florist shops, and most beds in nurseries have the makings of at least one miniature in them, perhaps five, or maybe fifty.

The first step, and one we cannot emphasize too strongly, is to train yourself to look for this small beauty. It can be found in so many more places than you would believe if you are not already a devoted student of miniature growth. It can be gathered from small plants where all parts are in matching scale. It can be young or immature shoots of large plants, which when fully grown later, would not be miniature material at all. It can be small fragments of larger plants. All this material does not have to be kept alive. Some of the most useful, can be dried and therefore almost everlasting.

SMALL PLANTS FROM YOUR GARDEN

Catalogs from nurseries specializing in hardy rock garden plants for your area will usually indicate size, and a sensible double check before you buy would be to go to see them during the growing season. Whether you grow them in your open garden or have a collection in a hidden corner simply to use for cutting, you will find most a fine source of miniature material.

One of the easiest to grow, and one that provides the most brilliant yellow of early spring is whitlow grass, *Draba bertoloni* and *D. bruniaefolia*. The wiry tufts of bright green, in the case of *bertoloni* covered with silvery hairs, provide wonderful foliage and the tiny flower heads bloom for weeks. The rosy-mauve fumitory, *Corydalis bulbosa*, comes even earlier than the drabas and has the most delicate racemes held above its turquoise, fern-cut leaves. The stonecrop or sedum family has many varieties that are in perfect scale for miniature arrangements and all last beautifully. They are especially a joy to use in shows where the air gets very dry and hot under exhibit lights. *Sedum glaucum* is one of the loveliest. The mats of blue-gray leaves shoot sprays of pearly white flowers in July, all no more than three inches high; *S. murale* has red foliage and white flowers and in *S. reflexum*, a great favorite of mine for miniature plantings, the bright green spikes have nodding tips and bright yellow flowers.

The familiar houseleek, *Sempervivum*, is another class with many useful varieties. Most have the hen-and-chickens look of sculptured rosettes and they last wonderfully well in both arrangements and plantings; *S. arachnoideum* is one of the strangest and most fascinating. The tight, small rosettes are webbed over with silvery filaments and the arching stems of orange-and-pink flowers are one of the miniature jewels of early summer. The skimpier the nourishment where they are growing, the closer these various sempervivums will stay to a useful small size for miniature work. It is therefore most practical to plant them in rock crevices or dry walls.

No one who loves small plants, miniature flower arranging and fragrant things (and they go together) should be without some of the thymes in her garden. The woolly thyme, *Thymus lanuginosus*, creeps close to the ground with soft gray leaves; *T. montanus album* is also a creeper with tiny white flowers. The most fragrant of all, *T. serpyllum*, the mother-of-thyme, has shining, dark green leaves and small spikes of pinkish mauve flowers that I have picked and used with pleasure from spring until late November.

For a really exciting color in a familiar plant that is perfect for miniatures, I urge you to grow *Viola odorata* in apricot. It is rare, beautiful, delicate and fragrant.

MINIATURE ROSES

Miniature roses, a delight to both grower and arranger, are surely the queens of the miniature flower world. Reproducing in their tiny flowers, often less than an inch across when fully open, all the beauty of form, color and sometimes the fragrance of a full-sized rose, they are indeed captivating (Color Plate 24).

Interest in them grows as gardeners and arrangers recognize their value. Nurseries which twenty-five years ago listed only a few varieties today offer among them more than 150, with new ones added every year. We now have whites, creams and yellows, the palest to the deepest pinks, all the reds you could imagine, a peach, a coral and an apricot-orange. We even have a miniscule lavender-blue. In flower form we have singles, semidoubles and doubles, pointed buds that are true miniatures of hybrid tea rose buds, others with all the old-fashioned charm of a cabbage rose. We have new varieties whose petals twist and quill. Bushes are often covered with flowers for most varieties are free-blooming. Although one hears of gardeners who find them good plants for indoors, they really grow best in the garden.

A mature miniature rose bush can measure from a few inches to eighteen, and its flowers from half an inch to an inch and three-quarters. Some varieties conform better than others to an overall miniature standard of small leaf, flower, stem and growth habit. Most pinks, reds and whites for instance, are consistently miniature in all their parts. In most yellows, fine foliage has had to be sacrificed for color, but work is constantly going on to develop yellows that will eventually have miniature foliage. Hybridizers are working on miniature climbers and standards with a few varieties already listed.

The ideal miniature bush rose, according to Clifford T. Wilson, Canada's foremost amateur miniature grower, is at maturity from six to twelve inches high and wide. The flower is from three-quarters to one and three-quarters of an inch in diameter. It has dainty, fernlike foliage with compound, serrated and closely spaced leaves, and the stems are fine and compactly branched. It is truly miniature in all its parts. Some growers list as miniatures roses which are larger in flower and coarser in foliage than this, but for arrangements or growing in a miniature landscape, we think Mr. Wilson's measure is excellent.

One often wonders how such things as miniature roses found their way into commerce and thus were set on the path that leads them on to our gardens. Clifford Wilson, who has delved into their history, tells me that the first recorded information about miniature roses dates about 1800 and is a painting in an album of roses by a Miss Mary Lawrance. Although records are vague, it is thought that the plants from which her roses came were from the Orient, the island of Mauritius or India, because of the species names in use at that time —*Rosa Chinensis*, *Lawrencianna*, *Indica*, *Bengale*. For some twenty-five years after that, several varieties were hybridized and distributed; then their popularity waned and they were forgotten.

About 1918 a Dr. Roulet came upon a little rose in Switzerland which he gave to his friend Correvon to propagate. A few years later it was introduced under the name "Rosa Rouletti." (Because the species designation is inaccurate, the *Rosa* has now been dropped in favor of plain Rouletti.) Except for those varieties which claim Oakington Ruby as their parent, Rouletti has been the breeding stock for most of our modern miniature roses.

It is to two nurserymen, Jan deVink of Holland and Pedro Dot of Spain that we owe some of our best modern miniatures. About 1935 both become interested in hybridizing these tiny beauties. DeVink introduced Peon, a bright red with a white eye, later renamed Tom Thumb by Robert Pyle of the Conrad Pyle Nursery, when he introduced it to the United States. More than twenty-five years later, it is still one of the best and is being used in its turn, as parent stock for new varieties.

DeVink went on to produce Midget, a crimson and white with clusters of small flowers; Pixie, one of the smallest, growing only four to five inches tall, with cabbage rose flowers in white flushed with pink; and a group of nursery rhyme varieties, Cinderella a shell pink, Sweet Fairy also pink and fragrant, Prince Charming scarlet and Simple Simon deep pink and very dwarf.

Pedro Dot introduced the first break in yellow, Estrellita de Oro —Baby Gold Star, and later a series named for jewels, Perla de Alcanada a free-blooming crimson; Perla de Montserrat a beauty with hybrid-tea shaped buds of rosy pink; and Granate—Garnet with bright crimson flowers and light green foliage.

Rose hybridizers in America have been interested in miniatures too. Ralph Moore has introduced, among many others, the popular Bit o' Sunshine, a rich, creamy yellow; and Dennison Morey is responsible for the dainty, pale pink Baby Betsy McCall, a top favorite with many miniature rose fans. We list other varieties that you may like to try in Appendix C.

If miniature roses are going to be used in show arrangements, it is well to cut them in tight but colored bud the day before, brush any you wish to stay tightly closed with a little raw egg white. Wrap all in a paper towel and stand in deep water until a few hours before the show. Bring to warmth any you wish to have half open, and when they are at just the right stage, brush the edges of overlapping petals with egg white and hold them in place until dry. You will find that unless the flowers are so treated, they will be full blown in a few moments under hot exhibit lights. This very thing happened to me with a show entry before I knew the trick with the egg white to hold bud shape. I made my arrangement with buds and half-opened flowers, and put it in place. Ten minutes later, and before the judges arrived, every flower was full blown.

SMALL WILD PLANTS

Nature is so bountiful you must hunt for wild miniature plants either in spring before they are hidden by bigger, ranker growth, or on rocky outcrops or shady places of the forest floor where nourishment is usually meager. In collecting those you have not grown, bear in mind, of course, the plants protected by conservation laws in your area. In spring, while snow still lies in hollows in the woods, you will find the creamy white Dutchman's breeches, *Dicentra cucullaria*, hung above ferny blue-green leaves. And where chilly rivulets of melting snow run over the ground, there are usually tufts of white and purple wood violets, *Viola odorata*, fragrant and small.

In woodsy places where soil is scant and growth sparse, you may find the vines of twinflower, *Linnaea borealis*, and partridge berry, *Mitchella repens*, their bendable leafy stems often as useful and lovely as their small-scale flowers. If not forbidden, club mosses, *Lycopodium*, ground cedar, *L. complanatum*, and ground pine, *L. obscurum*, have a thousand uses in arrangements and since delicacy can so often be sadly short lived their sturdiness is a constant joy.

On rocky places the sun is often hot, and here you will find mossy lichens and soft gray rosettes of the early saxifrage, *Saxifraga virginiensis*. Both are ideal for the base of tiny line arrangements to hide pinholders or other mechanics, and the saxifrage is also a delightful little plant to soften the harsh edges of a boulder or rock in a dish garden.

The common stonecrop, *Sedum acre* is a versatile plant for miniatures, with its fleshy leaves and stems and dancing yellow stars. This covers rocky hillsides in early summer with sheets of gleaming gold, but I have used the green parts of the plant, always truly miniature, throughout the year. A list of many wild plants for miniatures is given in Appendix A.

IMMATURE GROWTH

The possibilities of using immature flower buds or young shoots of larger plants that, when fully grown would be out of scale for miniatures, is almost limitless, for all new growth is at some time miniature. The shoot of a rolled-up leaf of lily-of-the-valley *Convallaria majalis*, will make a bold exclamation mark above a rosy wintergreen berry, *Gaultheria procumbens*, in an arrangement barely three inches overall. Birch or alder catkins could hang gracefully over a rim, or a rising curve of alpine currant blossom, *Ribes alpinum*, establish line and rhythm for a graceful tiny vase.

All the immature phases of ferns are useful—curled-up fronds in the early spring and freshly opened ones later, orderly green beads of the spore cases in midsummer. The world is full of such new young beauty as this and full too of people who would love to be taught to see it and to arrange it well.

FROM PARTS OF LARGE PLANTS

Whether you are walking down a country lane, down the aisle of a greenhouse, or along a path in a nursery, learn to look for plants, no matter how large, that have *something* miniature in their growth that you might use. In fields and woods, there are gleaming golden buttercups and foamy white meadow rue. There is meadowsweet, hardhack and goldenrod along the roadsides, sweet clover and blue vetch in the fields, herb robert and mountain laurel in the woods, jewel weed and cardinal flower in the damp places and pearly everlasting and tansy in the dry ones. There is nightshade and virgin's bower on the fence rails. Always you must abide by the conservation laws of your province or state, and always too be wise beyond laws about what you pick. There are blond seeds of cedar and frosty blue juniper berries, orange bittersweet, and scarlet rose hips, but beware those lovely chartreuse green pearls that are the berries of poison ivy!

The scarlet keys of the mountain maple have a hundred uses, and the prickly cases of beech nuts, the scaly pods of the ironwood and the tiny roses of the larch—there are a million, million things in the fields and woods for miniatures! We name here only a few. Fuller lists are included in Appendix A.

GREENHOUSE POSSIBILITIES

Greenhouses, especially those growing mixed crops, are still another storehouse of possible small-scale material. Double and single-flowered fibrous begonias, *Begonia semperflorens*—some call them tizzy-lizzies—are constantly useful and lovely (Color Plate 10). Many people, looking at a photograph of a miniature flower arrangement with a double pink or red begonia in it have thought they were looking at a peony. Blossoms of the crown of thorns, *Euphorbia splendens*, are a stunning bright orange with the dull bloom of velvet, and the vine, *Hoya carnosa*, has flowers with glistening pink petals and scarlet eyes (Color Plate 11). Both make the most dramatic accent for arrangements with a contemporary air. *Kalanchoe*, both creamy white and orange, and the new larger scarlet, is also useful. It lasts well and looks well under exhibit lights (Color Plate 17).

If you are preparing for a show when garden or wild things will not be available, be sure to search out greenhouse sources of miniature materials.

FLOWERS FOR MINIATURES FROM STANDARD PLANTS

Spring begins in our garden with one of the most exquisite miniature flowers even though it is on a bush ten feet high. It is the very early, *Viburnum fragrans*, and its pink and white, spicy scented flowers are the most welcome sight in the world. It may still be cold and windy outdoors, but to bring a little of this lovely shrub inside and make it into a delicate miniature where all the family may catch its sweet fragrance is a joy.

Flower Sunday in our church comes in early June and the children's bouquets are taken to a veterans' hospital nearby after the service. We always count on the dainty white stars of *Deutzia* and the pale pink of *Daphne* to froth up the little nosegays to pin on the pillows of the sickest patients, and johnny-jump-ups and forget-me-nots for small hand bouquets for the not-so-ill.

As summer floods into the garden we have the wonderful world of miniature annuals, the sweet alyssums, the baby zinnias, the tiniest marigolds, the pale blue stalks of lavender and salvia, the gay, bright-flag colors of verbena—there seems to be material for a thousand miniatures at every turn, and so little is enough! Trees as big as horsechestnut and thorn have exquisite miniature blossoms. The fringed lip orchids of the common horsechestnut, *Aesculus*, are some of the most exotic little things of the whole flower world. All in one panicle you will find some splashed with cerise, some with gold. The tiny double roses of thorn blossoms are also beauties, especially the variety Paul's Scarlet, *Crataegus oxyacantha*. In some areas it is possible to gather witch hazel tassels, *Hamamelis virginiana* and *H. mollis* in both fall and spring, and the flower of cornelian cherry, *Cornus mas*, is a golden burst in springtime too.

BEYOND FLOWERS AND LEAVES

For those who like the rhythm of line arrangements, there is material for all kinds of bold patterns. Grape and clematis tendrils never twist the same way twice. Pine needles, big or small according to the variety you choose, make a bold spurt of high line. Small tufts of tamarac burst off their branches like fireworks, and some of the most useful foliage comes from the smaller of the broad-leaved evergreens.

All the boxwoods, *Buxus*, are good and *Pachistima canbyi*, although not so useful a form as some of the others, adds a wondrous glossy green to mass foliage arrangements. In Zone 4, where I live, we are able to grow both the tiny *Euonymus kewensis* and *E. kewensis* Silver Gem, one deep green and the other a variegated silver-gray marked with cream and rosy pink. These provide cutting material the whole year. Such foliages last for weeks indoors with a soak under water every five or six days.

CONSIDER DRIED THINGS

There is no doubt that one of the tricky things about fresh flower miniatures is the need to replace water in the containers frequently. Because they are so small and can hold so little, the water evaporates quickly. For that reason, miniatures of dried material are great favorites with busy arrangers.

Flowers and leaves for drying can be gathered at any time, processed and stored away in plastic bags or small boxes. I have some favorite bits and pieces ten years old—eucalyptus seeds from California, many colors of immortelles, seed heads of columbine that swing on their stems like ringing bells, white heather from Scotland and a most useful little deep rose flower from California that I know only as the prairie rose. I use them for a few weeks, blow the dust off, steam them if they look tired, and then put them away for another year. More varieties for your list are given in Appendix A.

One word of warning—don't keep your dried miniature arrangements around so long they look tatty. Better nothing than that.

7.

Mechanics and Tools

LILLIPUTIAN counterparts of mechanics for large arrangements are needed for miniatures and a few tools to take the place of fingers when plant bits must be managed deftly. As with any flower arrangement, time taken to prepare a proper support pays dividends in good results, and also makes the whole experience of creation happier.

FOR LOW CONTAINERS

In flat dishes or open bowls, where there is usually no rim to brace wire or oasis, you have a choice of mechanics. If your container is deep enough to hide one of the tiny pinholders made especially for miniatures, you have only to see that it is firmly fixed to the base of the container with a little plasticine or, as many prefer, the sticky material used for caulking windows. Often you will find, however, that these miniature pinholders have a thick metal base and they therefore stand up too high to remain properly hidden when the arrangement is complete. A far better pinholder can be made by cutting one of the large, thin, plastic-based, standard size pinholders into small sections. You or a willing accomplice can do this with a hack saw or a power jig.

To make stems firm on the pins, wrap a small doughnut of floral clay around each and a little way up from the bottom, leaving the end clear to absorb water. Another useful trick is to insert fine stems into hollow-stemmed bits of stiff grass and press them down on the pins where you want them to stay, again remembering to see that the plant stem itself goes through into the water.

If the container is not deep enough to hide a pinholder—and many are not—there are other ways to accomplish your purpose. You can coat a sharp carpet tack with shellac or paint so that it will not rust when it gets wet. Then with a dab of plasticine stick it firmly to the base of the container. On it impale a little block of soaked oasis or aquafoam, and push the stems into that. If you want it to be even steadier, you can press one or two lengths of fine wire into the plasticine under the tack. Bring the ends up and over the oasis, twist them around each other to tie them and cut off the excess. You can make a whole little cage over the oasis in this way. This helps to prevent the chipping off of the oasis, as can happen if you push too hard into it with a stiff stem.

Since small amounts of water evaporate quickly, one of the main problems with fresh material miniatures is to keep the level up. A little block of oasis or aquafoam is even better than open water, for it holds moisture for a long time and provides support too.

In an open or flat container you may use for a holder a small spiral of copper wire or lead solder. Make this by coiling the wire around and around in a flat circle, fastening one end into the plasticine in the container. Then pull up the spiral, like a tapered spring to the height you need.

FOR VASES

When you use fresh material in vases, the best support is a tiny block of oasis or aquafoam or pieces of the crumby plastic material used by professional florists. Occasionally, to hold a bold line, you will need a little doughnut of plasticine around the stem. This should then be stuck to the back rim of the container.

Another useful trick is to make a miniature wire reproduction of the lead dragonfly which has been popular for so many years for holding heavy material in place in large arrangements. Fasten it, as you would its big brother, to the back rim of the vase with plasticine and bring the fingers forward one at a time, to bend around each main stem as you place it.

TO SUPPORT DRIED ARRANGEMENTS

For dried miniature arrangements, the mechanics are simple. Weight at the base to keep them from tipping over and support for your material are all you need. Fill tall or bowl containers with sand and when all plant material is in place, pour a little melted paraffin on top of the sand to hold it steady. Or press a small block of green styrofoam firmly into the container. If you have difficulty inserting fragile stems into this tough material take a hat pin, skewer or large darning needle and make the hole for the stem with it first. Don't take your eye off the hole before you get the stem into it, or you may lose it.

With flat containers, press bits of floral clay on the container wherever you want support, then push stems into it squeezing the clay together a little as they go in. If stems are too fine to be pushed into the clay without breaking, splint them first with a stronger stem or stick, or a piece of stiff, coarse wire.

A FEW TOOLS

You need only a few tools to make miniatures, but these are essential both to good miniatures and to your own peace of mind, and you will not be making miniatures long before you will want to find substitutes for the fat potatoes you call your fingers. I find the following items useful:

Tweezers, a pair of pointed and a pair of flat-ended ones

Manicure scissors with a long, thin point for pruning out undesirable material

Cuticle stick with a blunt end to press things into place, especially clay around dry stems

Eye dropper for watering

Fine, mist spray to keep material fresh

As you become more experienced, you will want some special equipment, perhaps a bundle of swab sticks painted brown to serve as extenders for too-short stems; another little bundle of pieces of stiff, hollow-stemmed grass for supports of weak stems; and of course,

(57) *Lockwood Haight*

ILLUSTRATION 57. ACCESSORIES AND TOOLS

Small figures, a pair of pottery lambs, a ceramic nun, an ivory fisherman, a crystal Venus, an Eskimo puffin, a Canada goose, a bronze snail, plastic lambs from the toy shop, bits of fungus, cones, moss and driftwood, twigs, stones, shells, bases are useful. For tools, tweezers, wires, eye dropper, cuticle stick, manicure scissors, tiny pin holders, clay, and fine sprayer are all that is needed. Author's collection.

different thicknesses of fine wires. If you are going to exhibit miniatures, the handiest carrier is a muffin pan. You can pack each arrangement in its own space, bracing it with tissue. Then pack the whole muffin pan in a flat box or shallow basket for carrying to the show. As we will explain, it is possible to make your miniatures the night before they are to be exhibited and stand them deep in water, one to each section of the muffin pan. By the next morning, they are fully turgid and ready to stand up well under hot exhibit lights for the whole day.

HOW TO STORE

Your equipment for miniature flower arranging is probably the simplest hobby material you will have to find storage space for in your house. A small cupboard, or part of a larger one, will hold enough to make literally hundreds of arrangements. I store my containers in rigid cardboard boxes three inches deep. I grade them as large, medium, and small and lay each size carefully in the box assigned to it on a layer of absorbent cotton or the packing that comes in candy boxes.

A lettered card, stuck to the front of the box indicates the size of container inside.

Similarly, accessories are divided by size, and packed in a softly lined box. Fragile ones, like a tiny two-inch madonna, or a one-inch crystal bird, get a special little box within the big one. Bits of tissue cup some of the china figures to keep them from chipping against each other.

Pill bottles, about one inch in diameter and two inches long, with squeeze-on plastic caps, are fine for bits of stone, cinders, precious things like agates, tiny shells, fungi. A slightly larger size is just right for driftwood and coral. Berries and cones go in these too.

Favorite twigs, branches and tendrils are kept intact by sticking them firmly in a block of styrofoam which you can either stand in a small box or hang up on the side of the cupboard out of the way. Or you can stick them by a dab of caulking around the rim of a bowl or cup.

Various sizes of wires, stilts and hollow stems for supporting, I keep in small frozen-juice cans.

Because dried materials are fortunately so light, they can be stored, each kind in its own plastic bag, in a largish box. Plastic bags will also keep glycerinized leaves in excellent condition. (By the way, never wash glycerinized leaves to clean them, it takes the glycerine out. Instead, wipe them with a piece of cotton moistened with more glycerine.)

PART THREE

Miniatures in the Home

8.

Miniature House Plants

An interest in miniature cut-flower arrangements leads to an appreciation of growing miniature plants indoors. It is so much easier to observe them closely, to appreciate their attractiveness, when they are near you as you work. However, the heat and dry air of most homes in winter limits the plants you can grow well indoors unless humidity is assured in a covered terrarium or glass bowl or by the perfect climate of a greenhouse or special case.

CACTI AND SUCCULENTS

Chief among tolerant plants are cacti and succulents, whose desert heritage makes them amenable to hot, dry air and whose relatively slow growth makes them easy to handle as miniatures. Forms are fantastic, and interesting varieties run into the hundreds. You could have an extensive indoor miniature collection of nothing but these weird little plants. Some look like thistle balls, some like spotted paddles. Some have the bold, geometric shape of pointed rosettes. Some look for all the world like small trees made of blown-up, pale green balloons. There is even one that looks like a green snake that has rolled in sticky stars.

(58) *Roche*

ILLUSTRATION 58. PLANTED MINIATURE IN AN EGG CUP

Rooted cuttings of miniature ivy and the gay-bannered, dwarf geranium Skies of Italy with cream, green, and orangey leaves make a bright miniature for a kitchen window or an invalid's tray. In time both plants would outgrow their miniature status, but in the meantime they make a cheery planter that will last for weeks. Height six inches. Arranged by Myra Brooks.

Surely there are no plants so strange in all nature. Collecting them can be an absorbing hobby and since they take little care and very little water, they are easy to look after. There are now many growers and greenhouses catering to this popular interest. Because cacti and succulents are so adaptable, they are shipped all over the country to auxiliary suppliers, and are therefore easy to find.

To set them off to advantage, choose a bold container. One with a rough texture often complements them best. For a collection that will be standing together, there is nothing better than a matched set of little pottery bowls or pots. Although the traditional pot with a hole ensures drainage, you can use containers that do not have an outlet. Be sure then that there is space in the bottom for at least one inch of sharp sand or fine gravel with a little charcoal in it. Plant your small cactus or succulent above this in the open sandy soil recommended for it. Water well after transplanting, then only sparingly, letting the soil dry out between waterings.

These plants will take all the light they can get, which often means a sunny, south window by day and then a dividend under a bright reading light on a table for the evening. This accomplishes two things. The plant grows better with this added light, and you can have the fun of seeing it nearby or close up, when you sit down to read.

MINIATURE GERANIUMS

No plant among gardeners is more beloved than geraniums, and no forms so popular as the miniatures. One greenhouse lists more than thirty-five, from the dark-zoned foliage and dark-red flowers of Merope to the green tiny-leaved, pink-flowered Tiny Tim. They are only two to three inches high for the first months of life, and one specimen of Tiny Tim we know is only a little over five inches at three years, and covered with flowers. Like standard geraniums, they require a sunny window if they are to bloom well, a cool spot, fifty to fifty-five degrees F., at night and a reasonably good garden soil, with sand added and sharp drainage provided.

There are more than a dozen varieties with double flowers and even more with single. I think the single flowers are a little large to be in the best scale for a true miniature plant. For this reason, I like the

(59) (60)

(61) (62) *Lockwood Haight*

ILLUSTRATIONS 59–62. MINIATURE GERANIUMS

59. North Star, white-and-pink single flowers; 60. Merope, the best deep red with dark-zoned foliage and double blooms. 61. Surely the tiniest gloxinia in the world, *Sinningia pusilla,* growing and flowering, lavender blue, in a one and one-half-inch bonsai pot. 62. Cuttings of the frilly, lemon-scented, chartreuse-and-cream Prince Rupert geranium, *Pelargonium crispum variegatum,* a charming planting in vermiculite and peat in a toy black iron cauldron with bird gravel for drainage.

proportions of the doubles better and prefer to grow them. There is one lovely little variegated geranium, Prince Rupert, pale green, with a yellow frilled edge, that you would love to grow just for its foliage and sweet lemon smell when you pinch it.

A MINISCULE GLOXINIA

The tiniest house plant I know, *Sinningia pusilla*, is a cousin of the gloxinia. A full-grown plant is no more than an inch wide and half an inch high, and the little purple-mauve slipper flowers are only half an inch long. It is the easiest and—although I dislike the word, in this case it is really apt—the "cutest" houseplant I have ever grown. You can forget to water it, the pot can be knocked over, you can transplant it two or three times in one week, nothing seems to bother it. I grow mine in a two-inch bonsai pot under the light of my desk. It never sees the sun. It repays me for my warm regard by blooming its head off all winter.

FOR TERRARIUMS, SNIFTERS, BERRY BOWLS

If you find particular pleasure in woodland plants, and would like to have them indoors through the winter to remind you of the fragrant, soft greenness of moss and fern, then you must duplicate, in your house, the humid air and peaty soil in which they thrive in nature.

This can only be done in a closed or partially closed container like a terrarium with a piece of glass over the opening; in a brandy snifter left uncovered sometimes but in a very dry house with a glass plate almost covering the opening most of the time; or in a berry bowl, which is simply a decorative glass bowl, often with a pedestal foot that lifts it above the table and a well-designed matching lid to top it off.

The list of wild plants suitable for such plantings includes nearly all the most beloved greenlings of our woods. Seedlings of hemlock, cedar and pine, the club and staghorn mosses, ground cedar, the tiniest of the ferns such as the polypody, cushions and carpets of all the mosses and little plants of violet, gold thread and twin flower are only some of them. For bright color, there are the brilliant, trailing vines of cranberry, the shiny green parasols of wintergreen with

(63) *Roche*

ILLUSTRATION 63. MINIATURE TRADESCANTIA

Knobby, long-legged branches match the lines of the legs of the flamingo, used here as a stimulating accessory. Pieces root easily in water, and thus compound themselves many times over. Arranged by Myra Brooks.

(64) *Lockwood Haight*

ILLUSTRATION 64. SOME THINGS TO GROW

Three planters with succulents, coleus, ivy and a budding orange kalanchoe for low accent at the base of a variegated treelike sedum. These attractive growing decorations last a long while in the house. Plantings by Eileen Spence.

red berries hanging beneath, and the paired leaves of the partridge berry with their bright scarlet terminal berries. These will stay fresh all winter. We have also been able to keep the green vine and white china berries of the creeping snowberry for weeks in such a garden.

CARE OF SMALL GLASS GARDENS

Not the least pleasure of such a garden is the warm smell of summer woods that rises to meet you when you lift the lid of the

(65) *Lockwood Haight*

ILLUSTRATION 65. CANADA GEESE

The theme of this dried landscape springs from the delightful pair of black soapstone Eskimo Canada geese, the female resting on the nest, the male standing guard. Coarse bird gravel makes the sandy shore, blocks of rosy quartz the rocks, club moss for a wind-swept tree, dried juniper for evergreens and a branch of starry sea lavender for a softening shrub. The container, a copper plate. Width seven inches. Arranged by the author.

(11) (12) (13) (14)

PLATES 11-14. IN FINE CONTAINERS. 11. A gold-and-white cloisonné pepper shaker holds a twig of cotoneaster and pink buds and flowers of velvety hoya with a miniature teak screen in the background. Height under four inches. Arrangement by Helen Murray. 12. White porcelain basket with the dainty Spanish rose Perla de Alcanada, and an infinitesimal mouse. 13. Royal Worcester gold-and-white jug with yellow roses, Baby Masquerade and Bit O'Sunshine. 14. Florentine silver open salt holding grass, wild dogwood, pink thorn and black privet berries. All under four inches. These three arranged by Barbara Ann Hynes.

(15) (16) (17) (18)

PLATES 15-18. WEATHERED WOOD, FRESH AND DRIED MATERIALS. 15. The container for this well-smoothed branch is modeling clay. 16. Colorful dried arrangements with buttons used as containers. Height four inches or less. Arrangements by the author. 17. Euphorbia, kalanchoe, alyssum and leaves of barberry and broom make gay entries for a May flower show. Height four inches. Arrangement in brown jug by Mary Baillie, in shell by Helen Griffin. 18. An eerily twisted bit of weathered wood on a base of storm-beaten driftwood. Accessories—the Mexican boy and the bird—complement the material and are in perfect scale. Height less than five inches. Both wood arrangements by Josephine Tyler.

(19) (20)

(21) (22)

PLATES 19-22. FOUR INCHES OR LESS. 19. Doll's cup and saucer of Spode holds a cascade of double spiraea, pink-and-blue forget-me-nots, purple lilac and tiny violas. Arrangement by Amy MacArthur. 20. A cut crystal salt dish sparkles with golden clover, waxy barberry flowers and the buds and leaves of Father Hugo's rose. 21. Still life with an ivory puffin that sits on a blue-grained granite chip to conjure up an image of the Scilly Isles, where rocks are soft with pink heather, wild honeysuckle and moss. 22. For a miniature vignette, a gilt chest – really a French jewel case – makes a setting for a flowered Chinese jar filled with pink honeysuckle and blue groundsel, with a pair of tiny figures and the mate of the container as accessories. Height of all, less than four inches. Last three arranged by Barbara Ann Hynes.

PLATE 23. AUTUMN BOUNTY. Vegetables and berries with bits of green foliage can be miniature too, as in this luscious, overflowing urn arrangement of cauliflower, broccoli, cranberries for rosy apples, privet berries for purple grapes, leaves of *Euonymus kewensis*, and stone-blue rosettes of sedum. A brussels sprout makes the cabbage-like base to which all are securely pinned. Height six inches. Arrangement by the author.

PLATE 24. THE FAIRY QUEENS. Almost too small to be true, these roses, hardly half an inch across, are miniatures of regular garden roses. Four varieties shade from palest pink to deep rose—Rosada, Cinderella, Baby Betsy McCall (a great favorite) and Perla de Montserrat. The container is a silver sugar bowl from a doll's set. Height four and one half inches. Arrangement by Barbara Ann Hynes.

(25) (26) (27) (28)

PLATES 25-28. LILLIPUTIAN MECHANICS. 25. Dried Queen Anne's lace, set off by a brass, shimstock screen is securely held on a black-button base by a dab of sticky clay. Arrangement by the author. 26. Hidden bottle top with a little pin holder supports a gay planting of euphorbia and boxwood with baby turtle accessories. Arrangement by Amy McArthur. 27. Little blocks of dry oasis or wads of sticky clay serve as mechanics for this bright trio with dried flowers. 28. A spiral wire spring anchored in floral clay supports a small composition with a wild white violet in a Chinese inkwell on a black button. All four inches or less. Last two arranged by Helen Murray.

PLATE 29. PERIOD PIECE. Portrait of a Lady. A brass, footed compote with a dried bouquet of clematis, fern and pearly everlasting on a button base beside a carved rooster offers a lesson in harmony of setting, container, flowers and accessory. Height three inches. Arrangement and painting by Helen Murray.

PLATE 30. PERIOD PIECE. Bouquet for a Doll's Dining Table. A silver bowl filled with grasses and May blossoms, that look like lush peonies, makes a centerpiece for a two-inch-high table. Flanking candlesticks hold minute candles and a cupboard displays little ornaments behind glass doors. Arrangement by Barbara Ann Hynes.

container. I have my best luck keeping such a garden in bright light but not sunlight during the day, and under a 100-watt light in the evening. Whatever lid I use—often just a piece of thin window glass —I place it so that a slit is open all the time. If I keep it closed tight, mould develops and some of the plants rot. This little opening lets the air move out when it expands with warmth. Moisture will gather on the glass, during warm periods, and then drop back on the garden again.

Only the lightest watering is needed, and then rarely. You can tell by the feel of the moss if the garden is drying out. We keep a pail in the garden for rain, or melt snow water in the winter when we do need water for them.

Much advice has been offered on soil mixtures for glass gardens, but I and my even more casual children have had great success with a green moss mat laid upside down over the bottom. On this is poured a mixture of pounded charcoal, peat moss and light garden soil, and in this the roots of the plants are tenderly but firmly placed. All is watered and left in dim light for two days, then brought to a place in the house where we can all glimpse it many times a day.

TO MAKE A WOODLAND SCENE

Even though the whole world is teeming with miniature plants flourishing in every field and patch of woodland once spring and summer are here, Nature's confusion or our own busy lives often prevent us from seeing their real beauty. So I urge you all when summer comes to have the fun of gathering some of the loveliest of miniature things so that you can enjoy them indoors. Because your house, at this time, will often be open to outside air, you will not have to worry about humidity. You will have to duplicate though, as well as you can, the conditions of light in which the plant grows naturally. Flat dishes and bowls are best for small woodland scenes. Although color in such winter gardens is restricted to green mosses and ferns and bright red berries, for a summertime garden you have the whole plant world of small flower and leaf to choose from.

When moving flowering things into a planting, try to catch them in tight bud. There is less shock from transplanting then, and by the time the plant is ready to flower, it has recovered and roots are re-

(66) *Lockwood Haight*

ILLUSTRATION 66. MINIATURE SUCCULENT

Crassula falcata, a thick-leaved, stone-blue rosette, planted in a turquoise bowl, and with three green-blue pottery lambs by Shimano, a fine Canadian potter. Photographed life size. Grouping by the author.

established. We have often moved mats of hepaticas with their furry-nosed buds into bowls to bloom indoors in a cool sunroom in April. Afterwards when they are through blooming we moved them to a spot in the garden. One clump of very blue ones has come in and out of our house every spring for nine years, and gets bigger and lovelier every year.

NATURAL SETTINGS

When you see a weatherbeaten mossy rock with a plant like a dainty wild scarlet columbine growing out of a crack, as you often do in the woods, you can immediately picture such a rock or boulder as a container for miniature plants. The rock can be lifted onto a tray that is then kept full of water to provide needed moisture around it, or it can be set in damp earth on a stone or concrete saucer or bird-bath and tiny plants grown in the crevices. Such a planting also needs to be sprinkled from above to keep it from drying out. With it you not only have a growing medium familiar to your chosen small plant, you have the dramatic contrast of its fragility against the hard, bold strength of the rock.

BARK AND DRIFTWOOD GARDENS

Although driftwood is often too dry to be a good planting medium for rooted miniature plants, pieces of moist stump or bark firm enough to hold earth and yet soft enough to absorb moisture make containers that have a perfect harmony with natural things. If carefully handled they will often last a whole season. Then the small plants can be planted back in the ground to be lifted again the next year and set up where they can be truly enjoyed.

We had such a bark garden for three months one summer on a table on our veranda beside an invalid's chair. Club moss made the tree; soft, low mosses the ground. There was a bit of stump with the scarlet lichen, *Cladonia cristata tella* so aptly named for the famous Grenadier Guards; some shiny pipsissewa, little ferns, creeping snow-berry and partridge berry, a velvety gray saxifrage on a dry rocky hump, and mushrooms and toadstools that were changed every few

(67) *Lockwood Haight*

ILLUSTRATION 67. MINIATURE HOUSE PLANT

Haworthia margaritifera has sculptured spikes of dark green with white spots, growing in a royal-blue Chinese inkwell. Photographed life size. Grouping by the author.

(68) *Lockwood Haight*

ILLUSTRATION 68. STRANGE SHAPES OF CACTI AND SUCCULENTS

Above left, bunny ears, *Opuntia microdasys albata;* above right, *Sedum pachyphyllum;* below left, *Echinocactus grusonii;* below right, the wiggly snake of the lace cactus, *Mammillaria elongata minima.* Containers are dark green, rectangular pottery blocks made originally to hold cigarettes.

days for bright color. For someone who for years had loved the woods but now could not walk in them, this was a charming treat. A word of warning—abide by conservation laws in gathering plants for such a garden, and always replant in the woods when summer is over so they may grow again in their natural habitat.

9.

Sink, Pan and Trough Gardens

WHAT an interesting study an anthropologist could make of the traits of character in different peoples that show in the way they express themselves horticulturally! What, for instance, is there in the Japanese that makes them such fine-fingered gardeners, so conscious of disciplined form, so appreciative of the textural values of foliages? What is there in the Englishman that makes him such an admirer of superbly grown masses of flowers, big and little? Whatever the reason, this difference is clearly noted in each country's use of plants in miniature landscapes. Where the Japanese bonkei and bonseki are scenes of distant mountains, winding or tumbling rivers, rhythmically pruned trees, in England the most popular small planted gardens are almost a magnified view of a corner of a private garden with masses of carpet plants, dwarf evergreens, even tiny rose trees all flowering as they would in a standard plot.

The containers most often used, discarded stone sinks and farm troughs, have given these little English gardens their names. First exhibited in 1923 at the Royal Horticultural Society's Chelsea Flower Show in London, these gardens are now seen at flower shows elsewhere, and are also increasingly enjoyed in private properties. Sometimes placed on a pedestal in an open, sunny spot, they are thus lifted up where it is easy to see each little flower and leaf. They are also used on balustrades framing steps and even as window boxes outside city flats.

The stone sinks and troughs are sturdy, a complementary soft gray color and, having a handy drainage hole already in the bottom, they make excellent containers for such gardens. They measure about thirty-six inches by fifteen inches, and are about four inches deep. If sinks or troughs are not available—and they are now becoming scarce—useful substitutes are often made from concrete.

Sink and trough gardeners follow the usual rules for good pot planting. A broken piece of pot is placed over the drainage hole, then an inch layer of sharp gravel added with a mixture of peat, sand and soil partially filling in above. A large stone, simulating a rocky outcrop, is set, more soil filled in and plants grouped around the rock. Books on these gardens generally recommend that a miniature tree should be the first plant to be put in place, then others added as the soil is brought level.

Although the design of most trough gardens is informal, it is possible with the same methods to make skillful small-scale reproductions of formal English gardens. Gravel paths, rose beds, tiny bulbs and plants carefully grown, even typical garden ornaments, a little fountain or summerhouse can be so cleverly placed that the best of these exquisite landscapes become collector's pieces and gifts for queens.

The list of material available in England for such plantings is extensive. Gardeners there have had a special love for small plants and have found great pleasure in growing them well ever since the famous plant collectors of the late nineteenth century introduced so many new varieties into the country. Although alpines at first were collected from the high meadows of the Alps, the term now refers to almost all low-growing, miniature plants, wherever they have come from. Many nurseries in England specialize in them, and there are literally hundreds of suitable varieties of trees, shrubs, bulbs and plants.

Interest in these gardens has already spread to America, and here and there gardeners are experimenting with growing plants in such limited settings. For those who would like to try this kind of garden-

(69)

(70) *J. E. Downward*

ILLUSTRATIONS 69, 70. ENGLISH PAN AND SINK GARDENS

69. A pan or, as we say in America, a pot, with earth, chipped stone and jagged rock, with mat growers, a flowering heather, a miniature rose in bloom, and a wind-tossed evergreen. 70. A stone sink planted with minute alpines, centered with a mountain outcrop.

(71)

(72)

J. E. Downward
E. B. Gilchrist, Jr.

ILLUSTRATIONS 71, 72. TUFA BOULDER AND TROUGH GARDEN

71. The rare and exquisite little *Jankaea heldreichi*, found in the wild only on the Thessalian Olympus in Greece, and very difficult in cultivation, here grows well on a tufa rock for Mrs. M. A. Brough of England. 72. An adaption of the English trough garden, made in a poured concrete container and showing careful placement of interesting stones with a small pine wired to develop pleasing shape, a tiny rose tree and the start of creeping groundcover alpines. Only a few months old, this miniature landscape was photographed in late fall. Planted by Ernesta Drinker Ballard.

ing, we recommend *Miniature Plants for Home and Garden*, by Elvin McDonald (Van Nostrand) and *The Art of Training Plants*, by Ernesta Drinker Ballard (Harper).

TUFA BOULDERS

An interesting material to miniature arrangers is tufa a curious spongy stone with a high limestone content, now also available in England. Gardeners have had amazing success in growing miniature plants in pockets of soil packed into these boulders, using them as one would a container. Mrs. M. A. Brough showed a rare *Jankaea heldreichi* in such a boulder at the Chelsea Flower Show in 1961. This little plant, found only on the Thessalian Olympus in Greece and very tricky to grow in cultivation, is doing remarkably well in such a boulder in Mrs. Brough's garden in England. Under her skillful care, it is flowering and setting seed. Such ingenious use of natural materials to create a lovely harmony of plant and container is inspiration to all of us even if we choose something less difficult than this rare little *Jankaea*.

10.

Decorating with Miniatures

MINIATURES are never a main element of decoration in our houses, rather they are grace notes adding character to the principal theme. They speak gaily of the owner's tastes and enhance the air of the whole house in a lighthearted way. Visitors feel that here there is an appreciation of beautiful, unusual things, for miniatures please everyone and always evoke a smiling response. And they constantly delight those who live with them, as any cherished and familiar ornament will whether it is an old family plate hung on the wall, a modern painting, or a bowl of favorite roses picked from the garden. For most of us, such personal enjoyment is the principal purpose of miniatures, and we may as well acknowledge this at the start.

Of course, their use can be overdone. Miniatures here, there, and everywhere on shelves, in niches, on tables and what-nots can be just as diddley as any repetitious ornament. They should only be used where they have an honest decorative purpose and add beauty to their surroundings.

For your personal delight, a miniature within the glance of your eye where its smallest detail can be enjoyed, will be the most reward-

(73) *Lockwood Haight*

ILLUSTRATION 73. WALL SET IN WINTER

Thin plywood shelves, painted cream to match the room, are hung from picture hooks, and miniature arrangements to suit the seasons placed upon them. The center and right set are dried materials, that on the left is fresh —species pink begonia, scarlet crown-of-thorns and variegated ivy, euonymus and hinoki cypress, pine needles, and a mixed bouquet of heather, wax flower, grape hyacinth, jade plant, privet berries, fern and podocarpus leaves. From the author's dining room.

ing. One strategic spot is on your desk, where you will see it as you write your letters, another on your bedside table for a last look at night, or on your dressing table for a first one in the morning. And most of us appreciate something lovely to look at beside the telephone where we so often find ourselves caught for more minutes than we like to count, or beside the kitchen sink for a small spark of beauty to lighten the jobs at hand.

Many arrangers find that this making of miniatures for their own pleasure at home is more stimulating than show work. No rules for size or schedule have to be followed, there are no pressures of time, no judges waiting, no concern to keep material exhibit-fresh. There is instead, every invitation to be leisurely, to play with new plants, to try new lines, new color combinations, to use treasured containers and accessories without any concern for their possible loss.

It is pleasant to experiment without having to buy expensive material. If you have never made an abstract composition, this is the time to try one—in miniature. If you have never tried a Della Robbia wreath nor a Japanese nageire, this is the time to try one—in miniature. Working in small scale, you can practice the techniques of handling flowers and thus free yourself for the spontaneous expression of your own talent later. Besides, it is all great fun.

GROUPINGS FOR DECORATION

To show off miniatures handsomely in your house, mount them on small shelves, much as you would exhibit them at a flower show. They can be framed or left open. I prefer them open, for frames large enough to enclose a set of shelves often dwarf the miniatures themselves. Such a set gives a wide scope in levels and offers a challenge to create variety in design at the start. The highest tier of shelves will lend itself to above-eye-level arrangements such as cascades and the dripping-down lines of alder catkins or privet berries. Middle shelves afford a straight-on view, and the lower ones are just right for those lovely little open water or sand landscapes that look best when you can look down into them.

A warning to the installers! Shelves must be fastened securely both top and bottom. Inevitably someone jostles them and proper fastenings are then the only insurance against disaster.

Shelves can be lighted from a spotlight hidden in a center fixture, built right into the ceiling, or by a picture light on a table beneath. If you should decide to set your shelves within a frame or box, have it built with hidden openings at the sides to install special tube lighting. Glass shelves, although they show every speck of dust, let more light through the various levels than solid material and make a stunning setting if light is cast up from below.

If miniature plants are to be part of such a set, they will more than likely have to be taken to the strong light of a window during the day and moved back to their setting later. Otherwise they will grow leggy.

EFFECTIVE BACKGROUNDS

You may find, as I did, that the color of a background wall rigidly restricts the colors of the plant material you can use effectively. Our first dining-room wall, where my miniature shelves hung, was deep emerald green. All dark things, including leaves and branches, were lost against it. Pale colors and white, of course, looked marvellous. The wall now is painted a warm beige, but we are still in trouble, for now the whites and pale colors are lost. The solution, I find, is to use miniature backgrounds that suit each arrangement. Such is the brass screen behind the Queen Anne's lace in Color Plate 25. Such would be the beautiful Japanese miniature screens that can be purchased as a set at the Metropolitan Museum in New York.

One dark background that shows everything well is black velvet. If your house is traditionally decorated, you may find that a simple, antique gold frame, backed with black velvet and with small shelves set in it, is a lovely way to mount your miniatures.

If the prospect of making six or a dozen miniatures frightens you (and I predict that it will not—when you once begin, only time will stop you), then put treasured small figures or ornaments on some of the shelves. And of course, for the long months of winter, the storehouse of fascinating dried material is best of all, and almost everlasting. Only a quick and gentle blow once in a while is needed to keep off the dust, and a light steaming every few months to bring back the bright original colors.

ILLUSTRATION 74. LEFT DETAIL OF WALL SET

Above left, a carved ivory vase with a species pink begonia; above right, variegated ivy and scarlet crown-of-thorn in a pewter vase on slag glass. (The penny indicates the scale.) Below left, a set of three mame bonsai containers; the left, a green pot with two stems of a miniature euonymus and a plant of hen and chickens; the center one a blue-and-white pot with a branch of *Chamaecyparis nana* pruned to look like a bonsai tree; at the right, a cinnamon-brown flat container, pine needles for line, bright orange immortelles for flowery accent and fine orangey-brown gravel. Below right, a silver salt with bits of pink heather, blue grape hyacinth, pink waxflower, jade-tree flowers and black privet berries; the foliage, podocarpus and leather-leaf fern. Arrangements by the author.

(74) *Lockwood Haight*

SECURE PLACEMENTS

Another word of caution. Put a little sticky plasticene or floral clay under each container and accessory and press down to fix them firmly to the shelf, for miniature containers tip easily. We had a strange mystery with the last set of dried miniatures in our house. Every morning, when we came down to breakfast, a mixed bouquet in a silver salt cellar, was lying on the table below the shelves and all knocked apart. I would repair it and put it up again. The next day it would be down again. Finally with some fancy sleuthing, we discovered that our cat was the culprit. Way down on the table below, she had caught the scent of the woolly leaves of catnip, and stretching to her tallest, she could bat the bouquet hard enough to knock it down to her level. I stuck all our containers down from then on and I never used catnip again.

PRESENTS AND PARTY FAVORS

"Minny-makers" will find many special uses for their talents. Party favors can be timely, as seed pod pins for an autumn party or wishbone bouquets for Christmas. Squares of pocket mirror bought at the dime store make a pretty mounting for dried arrangements

---

ILLUSTRATION 75. CENTER DETAIL OF WALL SET

Above left, a carved ivory Japanese fisherman catching a fish among reeds made from pine needles and rocks of shiny black coal. Above right, a pair of Canada geese, carved in green soapstone by Eskimos, and an evergreen tree. Center left and right, ceramic nuns, made in Italy, sing beneath a tree of bell-shaped seed heads; the symbol of the trinity, the eucalyptus seed at their feet; on the left, seed heads of wild columbine become amplifiers. The tree above the nun on the right is a seed head of Queen Anne's lace, the tree behind her, a seed head of silver rod, and the star, a bit of mother-of-pearl from a button. Below left, gray-blue Israeli vase holds dried goldenrod, leaves of yellow-and-green honeysuckle and dried bright orange mountain ash berries, The pricky sphere is a gray-blue globe-thistle head; bases are black plastic buttons. Below right, also an Israeli vase, in black with a spurt of beige, holds dried brown grass, white-lace seaweed at the lip, and a rose pink helichrysum flower at the base. Arrangements by the author.

(75) *Lockwood Haight*

used as place cards for a winter luncheon. Cards for Christmas or Valentine's Day can be two-dimensional miniatures, but use tough and thin plant material if they are to go through the mail, and glue them well.

A gay little bouquet on a present will sometimes be even more pleasing than the present itself. One of the best ideas for miniatures was a bouquet of dainty cones for the side of a knitting basket made by a small granddaughter for her beloved granny sweater-maker. That miniature won first prize for everything!

For invalids at home a miniature is an ideal present. A friend of mine, whose mother was ill for three years, made a new miniature for her breakfast tray every morning. Sometimes they were snippets from the garden, sometimes bits of house plants, sometimes cut flowers, sometimes rooted ones, sometimes dried, but always different. For her mother, who had been a keen gardener, the arrival of each new miniature was the highlight of the day, and far more delightful than a big bouquet.

ILLUSTRATION 76. RIGHT DETAIL OF WALL SET

Above left, a winter-gathered branch of sweet autumn clematis above a baby raccoon sitting on smooth river-bed stones. Above right, Austrian pine needles, supported in the holes of a dark brown button, repeat the pattern of the horns of an antique Chinese snail in bronze. The penny indicates the scale. Below left, bold twigs of horse chestnut with three cones of brown casuarina stand in a Danish wine cup, pebbled brown outside, blue inside, and thin as eggshell. Below right, a cliff of weathered sandstone shelters deer as they come to the lake to drink. Juniper and lichen grow in the crevices; the container, an ashtray, painted earthy red-brown like the rocks on the outside, and deep blue inside. Arrangements by the author.

(76) *Lockwood Haight*

(77) *Lockwood Haight*

ILLUSTRATION 77. FREE-STANDING SCREEN

A set of the smallest miniatures, the tallest a bare three inches high, are mounted on copper shelves on a linen-covered masonite screen—variegated honeysuckle and crown-of-thorn in a saki cup, pearly everlasting and juniper in a tiny basket; sedum in a footed blue-and-white vase; branches and pale hydrangea florets in a basin; fern and kalanchoe in another basket with an even tinier one for accessory; a chest of lycopodium and pepper berries with a rooster; a brown vase with clematis, box and waxflower; and a saki cup with coral species begonias, the penny indicating the scale. Arrangements by Helen Murray.

(78) Roche

ILLUSTRATION 78. PRESSED FLOWERS IN A DAGUERREOTYPE FRAME

Roses, lupine, yellow violet, and blue-eyed grass make a quaint, old-fashioned bouquet for a velvet-and-gold frame. The tiny corsage at the base is made of the pale pink miniature rose, Fairy, dried to perfection in silica gel. (Earrings indicate scale.) Composition by Myra Brooks.

(79)

ILLUSTRATIONS 79–81. PARTY FAVORS FOR CHRISTMAS DINNER

79. A tiny Christmas tree of gilded alder cones on a styrofoam base set in a bottle cap. Four inches high. 80. Christmas lapel pin, made with great ingenuity from seed pods, the tiniest of materials. Outside diameter, a bare one and three quarter inches. 81. Christmas favor, a real wishbone—or, as the dictionary says, a 'merry thought'—painted white and sparkled with a bow and a sprig of mistletoe made of seed pearls and germander leaves. All by Myra Brooks.

(80)

(81)

Roche

(82) *Roche*

ILLUSTRATION 82. PARTY FAVORS OR SALE ITEMS

Small dried arangements of gay flowers fastened with bits of clay to dime-store pocket mirrors make inexpensive and welcome favors. Above, dock and strawflowers; below, acacia with its own ferny foliage and strawflower with a candle. Three and one half inches tall. All by Myra Brooks.

(83) *Roche*

ILLUSTRATION 83. DECORATIONS FOR CHRISTMAS

Decorations from dainty dried materials for a ribbon-decked parcel, a bouquet of artificial fruit and strawflowers; for a Christmas card, pressed evergreen and dried red berries; for a Valentine, small hearts centered with a strawflower and wisps of acacia. All by Myra Brooks.

PART FOUR

Teaching and Exhibiting with Miniatures

11.

Teaching with Miniatures

MINIATURES are marvellous as a teaching aid for all kinds of people. Within the limits of classroom space, or a small studio, many pupils are able to handle a wide variety of material and not be too crowded to do good work—sometimes a handicap for standard workshops in flower arranging. Children have a special facility for little arrangements, perhaps because they are still close to a doll's-house world and intrigued by it. Also, when space at a large show is at a premium—and exhibition rental fees seem to be higher every year—miniatures can be used to teach a specific lesson, perhaps the different ways to dry and preserve flowers and leaves, and how to handle them once they have been treated.

And in garden therapy work with the elderly and the ill, miniatures prove both entertaining and practical. With only bits of material, a few small containers, a square foot or two of bedspread or table, the pleasure of making a lovely little arrangement or planting is as great as if one had greenhouses galore and work tables without number.

(84) *Lockwood Haight*

ILLUSTRATION 84. AN EASTER GARDEN

An indoor planting of miniature trees, paths and grass with the symbols of Easter—the Mount, olive trees, the tomb. Over the years, this has become a tradition for one family. Planting by Joan Robinson.

TEACHING CHILDREN

I first saw miniature fresh-flower arrangements used as a teaching aid with children about fifteen years ago. I had been asked to judge a spring miniature flower show put on by the pupils of Grade 7 and 8 (eleven to thirteen years) in one of the public schools in Toronto. There were more than a hundred entries cleverly placed on kindergarten tables, which were raised on kindergarten chairs, thus bringing the arrangements to just the right height for appreciative viewing.

Containers, as well as arrangements were made by the children. Beginning with blocks of preserving wax, they colored some with bits of discarded candles or crayons, and then carved out exquisite little

(85) *Lockwood Haight*

ILLUSTRATION 85. GAMBOLLING LAMBS

A little scene with moss, stone, an evergreen tree (*Juniperus chinensis blauuwi*), and sprouted carrot tops for the leafy bushes. Made by Cathy Wilson.

bowls and vases. A small knife was their tool, often just a school pen knife. With the cutting done, they rubbed them to a beautiful sheen with their warm fingers. For plant material, they used fragments of branches, little buds and flowers, some wild, some from gardens,

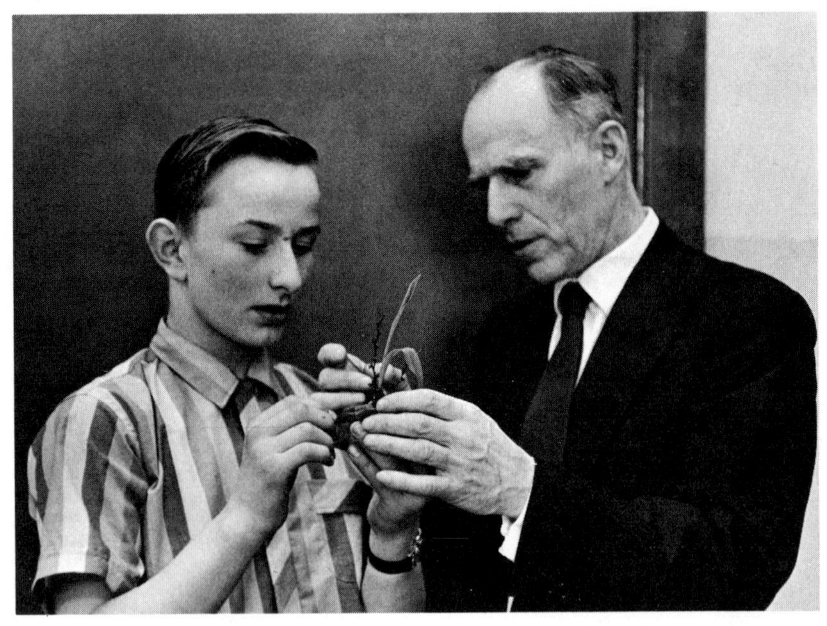

(86) *Henri Rossier for* Canadian Homes Magazine

ILLUSTRATION 86. A JUNIOR EXHIBIT

The former principal of Whitney School in Toronto, R. P. Montgomery, helps pupil John Edmison to prepare an exhibit.

but all in perfect scale and well handled. None was more than one and a half inches long or tall.

All the arrangements were good by the most exact judging standards, but the Best-in-Show that day was outstanding. The container was a small, soft, brownish orange leaf, and the arrangement a two and a half-inch branch, its catkins faced down with the tiniest yellow clover imaginable. Mechanics consisted of a little roll of copper screening stuck to the container with plasticine. The arranger was a twelve-year-old boy, a leader in the school, captain of the football team and a champion in chess.

The teacher of this group, Mr. Pat Montgomery, believes, and has through the years repeatedly proved, that miniature flower arranging is one of the finest ways to teach boys and girls a love of beauty, especially of growing things. His pupils are so enthusiastic they work in recess and after school, and often have to be reminded that it is time to go home.

(87) *Lockwood Haight*

ILLUSTRATION 87. PUPIL'S ARRANGEMENT

Lily-of-the-valley in a pale pink wax bowl, both made by a young girl in Grade 7.

During the years the Garden Club of Toronto was raising money to build and equip The Enchanted Gardens for Crippled Children, Mr. Montgomery, now principal of Whitney School, and his boys and girls, a different group each year, made an exhibit of miniatures for the Garden Club's Spring Flower Show. Their tiny loveliness and uncommon scale fascinated all who saw them, but of far more importance, the project absorbed and intrigued the boys and girls who made the arrangements.

GUIDES FOR A TEACHER

1. *Containers.* Many everyday things make ingenious containers —thimbles, buttons, bottle caps and so on, but we commend to you Mr. Montgomery's method of encouraging his children to make their own containers out of such a simple material as wax. (They must be warned not to leave them in too warm a place.)

(88) (89)

(90) (91)

Henri Rossier for Canadian Homes Magazine

ILLUSTRATIONS 88–91. CHILDREN'S ARRANGEMENTS

Boys and girls of Grades 7 and 8 in Whitney School, Toronto, made these containers and arrangements for an exhibit to raise money to help build The Enchanted Gardens for Crippled Children. 88. Shoot of lily-of-the-valley and wintergreen. 89. Line arrangements of barberry and arabis. 90. Beverley Baylay works on her little bouquet. 91. The finished arrangement, sugar maple blossoms, blue and white glory-of-the-snow. All less than three inches high.

(92) (93) *Lockwood Haight*

(94) (95) *Molly Bramley*

ILLUSTRATIONS 92–95. CHILDREN'S FUN

92. Ross Wilson makes a pie-plate garden as a setting for a pet toad. 93. A forest setting of juniper cuttings for a pottery baby bear. 94. Susan Adamson arranges wintergreen flowers and leaves with rosettes of saxifrage in a scarlet cup. 95. Hughie Redelmeier plants his treasures from the woods in a Georgian Bay Pie.

2. *Collecting Materials.* The boys and girls should be encouraged to collect and bring in much more material than an experienced flower arranger would need, for in the beginning they will not know how to use it economically. Much will be wasted while they are learning and experimenting.

3. *Preparation of Material.* They should be taught how to harden and prepare their material, making clean cuts and standing stems in deep water overnight, hammering woody stems, putting plastic spray on fluffy, fly-away material and so on. They should be encouraged to learn the correct name of each plant and something about its habitat.

4. *Tools.* Each worker will need a couple of simple tools, a pair of tweezers and manicure scissors (but not the ones from mother's dressing table).

5. *At the Start.* Pupils should not be taught or shown anything about known styles of flower arranging. It is far better to encourage them to develop their own. Gradually, as the class becomes more proficient and the practical problems of mechanics and such are overcome, it is a good idea to let the children analyze each other's work in front of the class, as adult arrangers do in their own workshops.

6. *The Goal.* Be patient, and do not expect miracles of beauty overnight. Often the best exhibit of the day is two sparkling eyes whose owner proudly displays a sticky bit of wax with a bouquet of limp flowers and drooping leaves.

GEORGIAN BAY "PIES"

For boys and girls of six to ten, making a Georgian Bay Pie is good summertime fun. The precepts of flower arranging are unknown to it. Its faults, if judged, would be glaring. One plant sometimes strangles another within the first week of the pie's life, or as happened in our house one year, the earth we used harbored a nest of horsefly eggs. To our horror, they hatched inside the house, all two hundred of them, within twelve hours of each other. However, even with such hazards, the value of a Georgian Bay Pie as a means of teaching small boys and girls the wonder of the plant world is without peer.

(96)

(97) *Henri Rossier for* Canadian Homes Magazine

ILLUSTRATIONS 96–97. WAX CONTAINERS

Variety in color and shape are possible with something as simple as wax. All these measure less than two inches and were carved out by the children. The color comes from crayons or candles melted with the wax before carving. The polish is the result of hand rubbing. Note the pin-holder firmly set, also the support of copper screening.

A Georgian Bay Pie (and you can name it after your own familiar summertime country instead of our Georgian Bay) starts usually with a picnic or at least an exploring sortie into a favorite hunting ground for the mosses, lichens, and fascinating small plants that are needed. Take along a basket for your treasures, or the very plate that such a pie is to be made on, so you can do your creating right on the spot, though this can be hazardous. Small fry coming home after an exciting search sometimes are very tired and inadvertently tip their pies, and the woodsy new gardens slide to the ground. As insurance against tears and heartbreak, we gather miniature materials for our pies in apple baskets and then have a making-up session when we get home. It is also not a bad idea to let gathering and making be a two-day project.

Materials for these pies are extensive, and little people, whose eyes are only three to four feet above the ground, are especially quick to find good things. Mosses come in a hundred different carpety textures. Little plants that creep, like snowberry or wintergreen, or stand erect like the false Solomon's seal, are easy to find. Lichens, such as the wooly gray caribou moss, are dandy for cushions to soften the edges of rocky outcrops. Tiny toadstools and fungi make fascinating accessories, and no Georgian Bay Pie would be authentic without a bit of rotting stump or branch covered with the frosty green of fairy cups and the scarlet heads of Grenadier Guards.

The making of our pies is one time when those who appreciate the principles of good design in the handling of miniature plants say nothing. The measure of a good Georgian Bay Pie lies not in its design, not in its container, nor in its line or mass, balance, color, or condition of material (which is usually pretty tired), but in the look in its maker's eyes. Such joy in the growing world, he will not lose so long as he lives.

SMALL GARDENS TO TEACH A LESSON

Often a little garden will tell a story to children which they will never forget. One family over the years, has made a tradition of building an Easter garden, beginning when the youngsters were small. Now that they are teen-agers, this continues as a beloved family custom, and the garden has come to mean more than just the Easter story for it is filled with little symbols of many of the picturesque events of the New Testament. Each one not only recalls the Biblical reference, but also its own story of how the family found it.

They begin by filling a large, shallow, oval pottery dish with peat, fine soil, and broken charcoal, mounding it up towards the center rear. This is the Mount of Olives, and on the peak are planted two little glossy green boxwoods, since these are close to olive-tree texture. Paths are made with bird gravel, and grass seed is planted on the soil. To one side a small treelike sedum becomes a tree for Zaccheus who, being a little man, climbed up to see Jesus pass by. On the other side is a miniature palm. Behind it quartz fragments make the tomb with an entrance stone, that is rolled back on Easter Sunday. There is a little wellhead and a pitcher where Jesus rested "about the sixth hour," and a basket for the loaves and fishes. A crown-of-thorns bush grows half way up the Mount and a vineyard of tiny ivy cuttings is planted at the base. There is even a bit of sandy shore with the ashes of a fire and a fish net spread to dry. Nearby lies a two-inch yoke that the family persuaded a French Canadian wood carver in Quebec to make for them when they found him carving habitant oxen with similar yokes.

Lately flowers have been added to suggest those of familiar Bible stories—bright bits of dried yellow yarrow for mustard, little bells of Roman hyacinths for lilies, heads of tiny immortelles dyed red and blue for the wild anemones that still cover the fields of Palestine at Easter time. With a mist sprayed over all each day and a light clipping of the grass with scissors when it gets too long, this little garden lasts ten days or more. The precious props are then packed away for another year and the plants tucked into a planter.

WINTER BIRDS

A little winter scene with a bird feeder three inches high, its feeding shelf about two inches square, can also teach a lesson. Grouped around the feeder are snowy evergreen trees with bits of flocked and dried tamarack tufts for bushes and a dozen or more of the birds we see in our gardens in winter when we put out the right food for them —a bright red cardinal, a blue jay, chubby English sparrows, a tiny winter wren, juncos, a red poll and brilliant yellow, black and white evening grosbeaks. Children quickly learn the habits of each of the birds, relate them to pictures and Audubon charts, and then go home to identify them in their own gardens.

Flocked evergreen is stuck into a styrofoam base, which has been

(98) *Lockwood Haight*

ILLUSTRATION 98. WINTER BIRDS

A garden scene, made to teach young children what birds to expect around a feeder in winter—chickadee, cardinal, winter wren, juncos, sparrow, blue jay, grosbeak and towhee—all less than an inch long, the wren less than half an inch. Birds modeled in clay from those on her own feeder and placed in this setting by Katharine Clarke.

scraped with a sharp knife to look like real snow. The feeder is glued from bits of balsa wood—the kind used for model planes. But the real fun, and an art in itself, is the modeling of the miniature birds. The smallest, the wren is, at this scale, less than half an inch long and Katharine Clarke, who made the garden in our illustration, nearly fell out her window a dozen times studying the wren on her feeder to get the correct posture of the head and the proper winter coloring. She modeled the birds of fine clay around a supporting common pin stuck into a cork, and used the plastic paint that comes in little bottles, both clay and paint being available in hobby shops. When the birds were completed, the ends of the pins were thrust into the styrofoam to hold them steady in the little scene.

12.

Teaching Adults

PUBLIC exhibitions of miniature flower arrangements or plantings are in a way teaching aids for both children and adults, since such exhibits have been the spark that started off many enthusiastic miniature-makers. There are also specific uses. The limited space miniatures need for a comprehensive exhibit; the small, in comparison to full-size exhibits, amount of material they require; the lower cost of gathering it and the ease of transporting it to the place of exhibition—these are all advantages.

THE ROYAL WINTER FAIR IN TORONTO

The first dried exhibit I was asked to make was a set of miniatures for the Flower Show of the Royal Winter Fair, Canada's largest agricultural exhibition. The purpose was to demonstrate the winter beauty in weeds and dried garden flowers to country women coming from all over Canada. To catch their interest, the flowers chosen were the brightest that could be found and the containers were all buttons, some flat, some bowl-shaped, some oval scoops. Thousands saw this exhibit at the Fair and many more, members of Women's Institutes through the country, heard of it afterwards in delegates' reports.

A few years later, in an exhibit of hundreds of different kinds of geraniums, also at the Fair, the committee of the Garden Club of Toronto, which arranged it, included a few miniatures. The interest in these little beauties was amazing. Everyone wanted to know about them, to know where they could get them. When an enthusiastic reporter mistakenly sent out a national press release about the exhibit and offered slips to anyone who wrote in, authorities were swamped with hundreds of requests. One farmer's wife even offered to swap a cow for a cutting of Black Vesuvius.

PERIOD AND STYLIZED ARRANGEMENTS

For the same reasons of convenience and economy, miniatures offer an excellent means of teaching the various historical periods and also the different styles favored to-day (Color Plate 29). This can be done with fresh flowers and leaves if the examples are needed only for one session; if dried materials are selected, demonstration pieces can be stored for use again and again.

One imaginative teacher has made small box frames to illustrate each period, and painted one-inch pictures typical of the period to go with each arrangement (Color Plate 30).

POSSIBILITIES WITH THE ELDERLY AND THE HANDICAPPED

Although we have been able to discover no one teaching the making of miniatures as a program for the elderly or handicapped, Professor Donald P. Watson and Alice W. Burlingame, authors of the recent excellent text, *Therapy Through Horticulture* (Macmillan), believe that miniatures would be a natural medium for such therapy. They demand no involved training for teacher or volunteer, they use little material, most of it costing nothing, they take little space to transport and lay out, they are neither heavy nor awkward, and best of all, they can be alive, which is in itself a special therapy.

The suggestions that Dr. Watson and Mrs. Burlingame make for the guidance of therapists with children, old people, convalescents, mentally ill, cardiac, deaf and spastic patients are the result of careful research and have professional approval. We recommend this book to all those planning horticultural therapy programs.

BUTTON GARDENS AS THERAPY

To make little gardens for others to care for is a therapy for those who create and those who receive them. Two enthusiastic button gardeners, Mrs. Florence Casebolt of California and Mrs. Harley Boutwell of New Hampshire, find their hobby wonderfully successful with hundreds of hospital patients and shut-ins, both young and old. Making button gardens at first for their own fun, they soon discovered that all kinds of patients found the greatest pleasure in learning how to keep such a garden green and growing.

Mrs. Boutwell, who has made more than six hundred of these little gardens in the last few years and spoken to five hundred groups about her hobby, modestly tells me it is easy to learn. She plans each garden to tell a story, a nursery rhyme perhaps if it is for a children's hospital, or something typical of a foreign country for an older person. She chooses a button, usually large like a coat button, and to make it steady cements it to a base—a caster cup or top of a cuticle-cream box. Then she cements a small ball of modeling clay to the button. When this is dry, she spreads the clay out and cements any background or tall material into it. Figurines or tiny ornaments are added next and little hollows made in the clay for the drop of cement and pinch of soil in which the live plants are to grow. Next plants are put in carefully so that no cement touches roots. If plants wobble, they may need another drop of cement to hold the tops snug against the background. Dried material is then added to fill in the design—stems of grasses, buds or seed pods and tiny dried flowers like immortelles or pearly everlasting. Little walks can be made of fine sand, and pools of hollyhock seed pods or acorn cups.

Favorite plants are the "pups" of sedum and cactus—offshoots that appear beside the mother plant. These grow slowly, need little care and come in fascinating shapes, colors, and textures. Seedlings of some herbs are also useful, particularly rosemary and thyme, and occasionally a tiny fern can be persuaded to thrive in a woodland scene. Mrs. Boutwell's button gardens and her own generous spirit are so well known that she has had to set up two greenhouses in which to grow miniature materials.

Figurines and other suitable little accessories come from the corners of the earth. Charms from bracelets and bits of jewelry, often from the dime store, are a constant source of pretty things, also tiny animals from gift shops. Odd bits of driftwood and stone, seashells and coral, nuts and cones, and seed pods are all bounty for the storehouse from which Mrs. Boutwell creates her charming gardens on buttons.

Care is simple. A drop of water when they are planted, and another drop every ten days is all they need. They do best without too much sun. Mrs. Boutwell finds that her button gardens last at least a year and she has one or two over five years old. Once in a while, a plant dies and must be replaced and most eventually must be lightly pruned to keep them small and in good scale.

Mrs. Casebolt, whose methods inspired Mrs. Boutwell to make her first button gardens, is the author of an excellent book on this delightful hobby, *Button Gardens and Diminutive Arrangements* (Florence Waye Casebolt, Alamo, California). In it she describes other intriguing miniature plantings in spoons and using weathered wood.

EGG-SHELL GARDENS

For shut-ins and friends at Easter time, Mrs. Boutwell also makes egg-shell gardens (Illustration 99). Breaking the shell so that about two-thirds remains, she removes the inside and paints the outside pale green, fills the shell with good garden soil plus a little charcoal, and places in it twigs of pussy willow and bits of interesting dried materials. A small bunny or chick is added and then one or two tiny growing plants. These are watered lightly and fine grass seed sprinkled on. This sprouts in a week to ten days. One shut-in friend faithfully kept the grass in her egg-shell garden cropped with manicure scissors and still had it growing four months later.

WE RECOMMEND. . . .

In working with those who are ill and helping them to feel the wonder of growth and to know the happiness of creating something as beautiful as a miniature, we have learned in the little we have done, that it is important:

1. To arrive when we are supposed to, and with our material well organized.

(99) Swenson

ILLUSTRATION 99. PLANTED EGGSHELLS

For shut-ins at Easter, two plantings with twigs of pussywillow and dried seeds, succulents and real grass growing; bunny or chick for an accessory and a white button glued to each egg for a steady base. Made by Mrs. Harley Boutwell.

2. Not to set too high a standard or have too long a session of work—after all, our mission is accomplished if the patient is cheered and feels he has done something worth while, not whether we think he has made a Tricolor.

3. To be careful about making a mess. Take a plastic sheet to put over the bed, or the table and the bed or lap. Carry material in a rack made for glasses, but with small frozen juice cans to use as containers and these only partly full of water so as to avoid spilling. A block of oasis in each to hold both stems and water is a convenience. Stop before the patient tires, and in plenty of time to pick up bits and pieces.

4. To bring to the very ill a little bouquet, not too fragrant, the stems wrapped in a piece of damp facial tissue and Saranwrap. Pin this low on the pillow where it can be seen without moving the head or held in the hand.

5. Not to expect anyone to thank you, just be glad that you are the lucky messenger bringing small mysteries.

13.

How to Exhibit Miniatures

No matter what intriguing classes a Flower Show Schedule presents, if there are miniatures in it, these will be the most popular classes with the public. They Oh! They Ah! They gaze with sheer delight. This is a change from the usual attitude of visitors who confronted with full-size arrangements feel they must stand back for a critical view, weigh the correctness of the judge's decision, the exhibitor's good or bad taste, her skill in handling material, or her lack of it. When they come to the miniatures, all is perfection, all is enchanting. For the exhibitor, this enthusiasm is stimulating, but she must still give close attention to schedules and rules to promote good competition and fair judging.

AUTHENTIC SIZES

The official *Handbook for Flower Shows*, prepared by the National Council of State Garden Clubs is generally accepted by show committees in North America as the authority for miniature classes in flower shows. It sets an overall five inches, either way, as the standard measure. At one time three inches was the measure of a miniature. Later this was increased to four inches. But this proved a difficult size to stage and by the time necessary barriers were set up to keep the pokers and feelers among the visitors from damaging the exhibits, to say nothing of ladies with broad-brimmed hats, the public was too far away to enjoy the beauty of such tiny creations. The smaller size also put a difficult limit on the use of fine containers, and these are always half the charm of a good miniature arrangement. The official measure was therefore raised to five inches.

STAGING FOR MINIATURE CLASSES

The creation of a tiny perfect flower is one kind of beauty; for man to make a tiny ornament to hold it is another. And for an inspired flower arranger to bring the two together and present them where they can be seen and enjoyed by hundreds of people, is perhaps the ultimate perfection of both. This requires not only an observant arranger but a clever staging convener as well. No matter how skillful the exhibits, if the staging is not attractive and suitable, all is lost.

I have seen flower shows where the miniature classes were staged in heavy gilt picture frames with black velvet backgrounds, eight exhibits to a frame; where the staging was a three-tiered set of glass shelves, five feet long, holding nearly twenty entries; or a series of painted metal, individual shelves each supported with a plaster feather, and another series of similar shelves supported with a thin, black iron S for a bracket. Each of these sets imposed some handicap on the arranger, for the exhibit was inevitably viewed by the public as an entity, and it was difficult to isolate one arrangement and see it as a whole, even on an individual shelf.

For the last three years the Spring Flower Show of The Garden Club of Toronto, long famous for its delicate miniatures, has exhibited each in an individual circular or oval niche, a setting first used, I believe, at the International Flower Show in New York. These little portholes, six inches in diameter and four inches deep, are cut in a solid wall. This construction hides the shelf supports and the mechanics of lighting. I think it is the best miniature staging I have seen or exhibited in.

The Toronto set holds twelve exhibits in all. Depending on how tall you are, the circular spaces are either slightly above average eye level or slightly below. The only disadvantage is that the round porthole sets a strong line to enclose the arrangements and gives an ad-

(100) *Herb Nott*

ILLUSTRATION 100. WALL SET FOR A SHOW

An exhibit using an indented box indirectly lighted and with simple copper brackets and shelves. Arrangements by Josephine Tyler.

(101) Roche

ILLUSTRATION 101. MINIATURE NICHE FOR A SHOW

A dramatic setting with each tiny arrangement given its own space. The curve of the niche suggested the main line of this design with buds, leaves and fruit and more berries spilling down the base. Arranged by Myra Brooks.

vantage to those choosing circular or sweeping rhythmic lines in their containers and materials. This is really not too serious. The important thing in staging is to keep the whole exhibit area in such scale that the minuteness of the miniatures themselves is enhanced and not overpowered.

The best staging for miniatures makes all supports and surrounding walls subordinate to the arrangements. It should be fine featured, well lighted, preferably from above, and each exhibit should stand far enough away from other exhibits to establish its own scale. Shelves, one directly above the other, seldom make a good exhibit; one level, usually eye level, is more pleasing for most entries since that will be the height the exhibitors have planned them for. The other levels, some higher, some lower, will not show to best advantage exhibits that have been planned and made to be shown at eye level. Exhibitors often feel, when this happens, that they are showing at a disadvantage, and this does not promote the good spirit of show. Also, shelves below the top one are seldom well lighted because of shadows cast on them from above.

As we have mentioned before, large picture frames, so often a choice for showing miniatures, rarely make a good unit. They have to be carefully chosen if they are not to dwarf the small scale of the miniature themselves. Individual niches are really much better.

ATTRACTIVE BACKGROUNDS

Whatever the set, it should be painted in a well-chosen background color. If, as often happens, there is one background color used for the whole show, this will, more often than not, also be complementary to miniature material. Soft gray is the most popular, with celadon green running a close second. But I have also seen stunning miniature classes done against a stony turquoise blue, a dusty grape purple, a bronzy black, and, once, a glistening Christmas set against dull gold. As in other classes for show, the staging convener should see that each exhibitor is given a sample of the chosen background color against which to plan her entry.

SIGNS AND BARRIERS

Signs needed to identify the class, the exhibitor, the plant material, and to hold winning ribbons should be fixed to the set so that they do not detract from the much smaller size of the exhibit itself. This is easy to do, if generous space is left between exhibits, and if the pattern of this necessary information is carefully planned when the whole exhibit is originally designed.

Also, if the viewing public compulsively pokes and pinches the flowers in the full-size classes of arrangements in the rest of the show —and nearly always they do—they will poke and pinch miniatures even more. Whatever is being planned in the way of ropes, rails or barriers to keep people from handling exhibits in the rest of the show, should be doubly provided for the miniatures!

HINTS FOR EXHIBITORS

On Scale: In many years of miniature exhibiting, I have seen more flower arrangers washed aground on the rocky reefs of scale than on any other of the measures of a good miniature. Sometimes it is the simple proportion of the arrangement to its space. This, as in larger arrangements, is almost a matter for mathematical reckoning. The arrangement should occupy not more than two-thirds of the space allotted to it, and I have seen far more first prizes go to miniatures that occupy less rather than more. There is something dramatic and appealing about plenty of clear space around a beautiful little miniature.

Use of Space: As with standard arrangements, the wise exhibitor will make a dummy of the space her miniature will occupy so that she may practice in it (Illustration 104). She will fill in the approximate color being used for the background of the set in the show, and reproduce, as well as she can, the lighting. Then on her practice stage set, she will work out at home the best exhibit she can, always being careful to conform to the specifications of the schedule.

Conditioning: Plant material should be hardened well ahead, for wilting and dying occurs with improperly hardened miniature material even faster than with large flowers and leaves. Tiny containers that hold only a little water add to this hazard. My favorite method for preparing miniatures for exhibition is, first of all, to soak all flowers up to the head and all foliage completely in warm water, in a cool place for a few hours. Then I make my arrangements the evening before and spray with a fine mist. Next, I stand the container, flowers and all, in a small dish with water deep enough to come up

(102) *Roche*

ILLUSTRATION 102. FRESH AND DRIED ARRANGEMENT

A glass shelf holds a grouping of miniature passion vine (for line), rose buds, and geranium foliage, all fresh, and purple and pink salvia, pearly everlasting and white statice, dried. Arranged by Myra Brooks.

over the rim. I lay a thin layer of facial tissue (split an ordinary piece in two) over the top and spray it. Finally I place the whole thing in the refrigerator, or in a cool room for the night.

Stands: Miniatures, as well as larger arrangements, are enhanced by a well chosen, appropriate base. The space for a miniature exhibit should be treated as the frame of a still life, the bottom of the exhibit space being just as important as the other boundaries. Let there be no mistake, entries planned with this in mind, win ribbons. Stands, lovely ones in muted colors and intriguing shapes come a dime a dozen almost in button departments and from the tops of old perfume bottles. Or they can be made from bark and wood, or even old records, as we suggested in Chapter 5. Tiny patches of lovely fabrics make delicate mat bases, and can be cut from remnants of dress material and ribbon.

Accessories: Miniature accessories in arrangements often stop the show almost more than the flower arrangements themselves. There is only one word of warning I must insert here. Do not, if you are showing in a miniature class open to the public, use any treasure that could not be replaced, and be sure to fasten even the replaceable ones down to the base if you value them. Such tiny things are easily stolen, and seem to produce an almost uncontrollable urge in the light-fingered to practice their talents. Oddly enough, I have never heard of a container being stolen, only accessories.

Stability: When all is gathered and put in position, it is the wise exhibitor who sticks everything down with floral clay, or even, in the case of accessories and stands, with quick-drying, transparent glue. Many a miniature exhibit in a flower show has been jolted by a last minute, good-hearted, but heavy-handed adjustment to lighting or support. Two or three of the most delicately balanced exhibits can, as quick as a wink, start their public life flat on the floor. This has occasionally been known to improve the design of the exhibit, but it never improves the nerves or the good temper of the exhibitor.

Transporting to the Show: Some schedules require that all arrangements be made at the show, others do not. Certainly it is easier to create miniatures in the quiet of your own house. You can then carry them, completed, or partially completed, to the show. This is much better than trying to make them from scratch in the hurly-burly of set-up time before an opening, when your wrists feel like jelly and your fingers about as dainty as an elephant's trunk.

When it is time to pack up to go to the show, I set my miniatures in a bed of absorbent cotton or facial tissue in one section of a muffin pan, wadding soft "doughnuts" of more cotton or tissue around them to brace them firmly. In other sections of the muffin pan, I carry spares of my plant material, in case of accident to the original. These are sometimes just floating in water, sometimes poked into a small piece of saturated oasis or aquafoam. One or two of the spaces will also carry tools that may be needed—manicure scissors, tweezers, bits of fine wire, clay, an eye dropper for watering.

Once, when I was taking a set of fresh-flower miniatures to a show as a special exhibit illustrating the history of flower arrangement, I carried twenty arrangements, five inches and under, in this way. It took only a few minutes to give them finishing touches and set them in place.

If your schedule calls for making all arrangements, including miniatures, at the show, you would be wise to follow the same plan of hardening, making, and cooling overnight. Then, in the morning, lift out your material carefully and pack it with spares, either in a muffin pan or small box lined with wax paper and moist absorbent cotton.

Working at the Show: Check the mechanics, and if necessary, replace anything that is loose or, as oasis can be, too fractured to be useful again. Efficient mechanics are even more important for a tiny miniature than a large arrangement.

Also take with you, to the show, a sturdy cardboard box to give you a working surface raised twelve inches or so above the show table. Then get yourself a chair, even if you have to steal it from under the exhausted staging convener, pretend that you have suddenly gone deaf, and concentrate on putting your miniature together.

SCHEDULE FOR MINIATURES

Almost any specification that makes a good show class in standard arrangements makes a good miniature class. Themes can be inspired by the container—pottery, glass, copper, silver, stone. They can be tied together by style—Japanese, Georgian, natural, contemporary. They can be all dried material, or all fresh, or a mixture of both. They can call for a container with a common use—open salt cellars, liqueur glasses or buttons.

(103) *Lockwood Haight*

ILLUSTRATION 103. THREE ARRANGEMENTS FOR AN EXHIBIT

For a few miniatures in a larger exhibit different levels of bases are used so that each arrangement can stand alone. Here, a plain oak block, rubbed with black paint, forms the main base. Each arrangement then has its own fitted base, and a block of dry oasis holds the center one above the other two. Below left, lily-of-the-valley, white violets and ivy cluster around a piece of slag glass; center, lily-of-the-valley, white grape hyacinth, rock phlox, johnny-jump-ups and maple flowers; below right, corky twigs of Boston ivy with florets of Jeanne pink geranium. Arrangements by Barbara Ann Hynes, Eileen Spence and the author.

Often a show will have a main theme that will suggest a companion miniature class. The Spring Flower Show in Toronto one year used *Time* as its main theme, with standard classes on *Time for Elegance*, calling for a fine container; *Time for Economy*, a thrift class; *There'll be a Hot Time*, all red and so on. The miniature class was *Time for Little Dreams*, calling for an airy arrangement suggesting fantasy. Another year, the theme was *The Arts*, with classes on the symphony, the ballet, the art gallery and museum. The miniatures were *The Minor Arts* stressing beauty in hand-made containers.

To call for arrangements with one kind of plant predominating makes a harmonious exhibit. Succulents are an interesting group for such a class, and if the show comes at the right time of the year and enough members grow them, a class in miniature rose arrangements is lovely.

Children love classes that call for the figure of an animal as an accessory, and these are always easy to find. I have thought too, although I have never seen one, that a fascinating miniature class could be made with chess men as the dominating accessory.

And everybody loves a challenge class. This can be most successful if it is a container, perhaps a coaster, that is the same for everyone and given out ahead of time, each exhibitor to make her arrangement at home to a common specification.

It is also possible to have a good challenge class by following the plan used for standard classes where a similar container and box of plant material is given out to half a dozen exhibitors who see it for the first time on the morning of the show. They proceed to make their exhibit right there, before everyone. This, however, will only work if the exhibiting group for the show has an experienced number of miniature-makers who are not already working on fifty other committees. Miniature-making in public at a flower show is, to say the very least, difficult and should only be attempted by the most tranquil.

SCORING AND AWARDS

Scale, as we have said—but never too often—is the most important element in the design of a miniature. This means the scale of the plant material to the container, the scale of the various kinds of plant material to the space and to each other. As the National Council *Handbook for Flower Shows* states, "Miniature arrangements and/or compositions reproduce in miniature the effect (in container, plant materials and accessories, if accessories are used) of artistic exhibits of larger size. The fundamental principles of design apply to miniatures, the same as to all larger designs, with scale the most important of all the art principles. Flowers, foliage, container, base and accessories if used, must be very small in size. Plant materials must, by their natures, be relatively small in scale."

The recommendation for scoring in *The Encyclopedia of Judging and Exhibiting* by Esther Veramae Hamel is:

Scale	40
Design	25
Color	15
Condition and suitability	10
Individuality	10
	100

I cannot overemphasize the need for all exhibitors of miniatures to choose flowers and leaves that are truly miniature and to handle them in their exhibits as tiny counterparts of a larger arrangement. As we said earlier, it is not regarded as quite cricket to change your material into miniature scale by pulling off petals, trimming with scissors or generally fooling around with the original flower or leaf. If, however, it makes you feel creative and you want to take the chance that the judge will not be sharp enough to see what you have done, that is your privilege. You will still, of course, have to face the jury of your other exhibit mates and, in the long run, their respect and admiration could well mean more to you than a first ribbon.

Of the other qualities looked for by judges in scoring miniatures, design, balance, relation of plant material to container, color, condition of plant material, all follow the same principles that make for good, standard arrangements. Perhaps one of the main challenges that intrigue arrangers of miniatures is that all these principles must be applied in such a tiny space and with living flowers and leaves that must be kept alive and fresh with only a few drops of water. There is something in all of us that is stimulated by challenges like these.

Judges usually award ribbons as in other classes to miniatures. There is, however, a present ruling of National Council that no miniature shall be considered for the Tricolor or the Award of Distinction or the Award of Creativity. From the point of view of the general public, such rulings are probably wise, since a miniature arrangement might not seem important enough. Being a miniature admirer, however, leads me to prefer the ruling of The Garden Club of Toronto, which at their big flower show of the year allows miniatures to be considered for the top best-in-show award, the Founder's Gold Cup. Although no miniature has won this award in the years the show has been held, there have been runners-up.

CHECK LIST FOR NEW EXHIBITORS

1. Read the schedule carefully, and if there is ambiguity, call the convener of your class and have it clarified.

2. If rules permit, make your miniatures at home ahead of time and put only the finishing touches on at the show. If they do not, plan your exhibit at home, take it apart for carrying and put it together again at the show.

3. At home make a dummy of the show space, using the exact measurements and shape, copying the background color and lighting. Practice in it at home.

4. If the exhibiting space is a niche, or circular opening, remember that this will frame your arrangement with a strong line which you should consider as part of the auxiliary design of your arrangement.

5. If the exhibiting space is a large frame, or a large open set, know that your arrangement can be of bolder material than if it is contained in an individual space. A very delicate arrangement is often lost in a large open exhibit, or if it is one of a series encircled by a heavy frame.

6. Be sure to leave clear the proper proportion of occupied to unoccupied space.

7. Keep plant material, container and accessories within the allotted space; do not let them protrude beyond the opening nor touch the sides.

8. Consider that bases are included in the overall measurement. If you use them, check total height and width.

9. Check mechanics to be sure that all is secure.

10. Check water supply in the container (once I did not, and all was wilted when the judges arrived!).

(104) *Lockwood Haight*

ILLUSTRATION 104. EXHIBIT SPACE

Dummy of space for a show makes it possible to practice at home in an area of the exact size to be provided. A fibreboard box with plug and extension wire, the background painted the proper color for the class, is invaluable for both novice and expert. This five-inch miniature in a footed one and one-half inch cup has pink heather for the curving line, white alyssum and rosy baby zinnias for mass, catnip for foliage. Arranged by Georgina Bryden.

11. Plan to arrive at the show in plenty of time to set up your exhibits and repair any travel damage.

12. Lay facial tissue on the shelf around the container while you make last-minute touches and add the last drops of water—paint used for flower show sets is often pale and of dull finish, showing water stains easily.

13. Check your exhibit during the show and add water as necessary.

14. Stick or glue your container and accessories to the base to prevent stealing and the whole arrangement to the shelf to prevent falling. Do not use irreplaceable treasures as accessories.

15. Do not count on pale blue or lavender to hold true color under artificial light. They fade. Bright blue is a better choice.

16. Harden your material carefully and carry spares to the show in case you need them. If the show lasts overnight, plan to replace all delicate material daily.

17. After the show, remove exhibits promptly. It is not fair to expect your staging convener, nor your class convener, to look after your tiny things.

18. Remember that the important thing is not who wins ribbons, what the judges comments are, nor what people say. The important thing is that you have enjoyed being a miniature-maker.

Appendix A

Materials Suitable for Miniature Arrangements

THESE lists are made up with plants that are hardy for Northern New York State and Eastern Canada, Zone 4. If you live in another area, it would be wise to check names and varieties with a reliable source of hardy plants for your zone.

EVERGREENS

Andromeda
Pieris japonica, for waxy, cream flowers.

Box in variety for small foliage, good green and long lasting.

Broom in variety for strong line foliage.

Cedar in variety for foliage and seed heads, especially *Thuja occidentalis*, Little Gem, to train for dwarf tree.

Cotoneaster in variety, for foliage and berries, especially *Cotoneaster dammeri*, which also has small white flowers.

Cypress in variety, especially
Chamaecyparis nootkatensis pendula, the Weeping Nootka False Cypress, for its foliage and seeds.

Chamaecyparis pisifera filifera, for foliage.
Chamaecyparis pisifera filifera aurea, for golden foliage.
Chamaecyparis obtusa nana, the Hinoki Cypress, for lovely green fan-like foliage, most useful.

Euonymus in variety, small tips and foliage of
Euonymus fortunei acuta, Silver Gem, flushed with pink.
Euonymus fortunei acuta, Woodlandi, miniature, glossy green.
Euonymus radicans minimus (*kewensis*) very small leaves, long-lasting.

Firethorn
Pyracantha coccinea, Kasan
Pyracantha coccinea, Lalandei, both for orange berries.

Garland Flower
Daphne cneorum, glossy foliage and fragrant pink flowers.

Heathers in variety, especially
Erica carnea, King George, good foliage and lovely flower bells in perfect scale.

Hemlock
Tsuga canadensis, for its tiny cones.

Hollies in small-leaved variety, especially
Ilex crenata, glossy leaves, black berries.

Ivies in variety, small tips.

Juniper in variety, especially
Juniperus chinensis blauuwi, compact, makes excellent conical evergreens for miniature landscapes
Juniperus plumosa, the Andorra juniper, purplish in winter

Mountain Laurel
Kalmia latifolia, for pink and white flowers.

Oregon Grape
Mahonia aquifolium, for its yellow waxy flowers and bloomy blue berries.

Pachistima
Pachistima canbyi, good foliage, but not superlative.

Periwinkle
Vinca minor, for tips of trailing creepers.

Pine in variety for their needles.

Yew in variety, for small new tips and red berries.

TREES

Birch in variety
Betula, for buds, immature leaves, tiny catkins.

Hawthorn in variety
Craetagus crusgalli, white flowers and red fruit.
Craetagus oxycantha, Paul's Scarlet, rosy scarlet flowers, double.

Horsechestnut
Aesculus glabra, with greeny-yellow flowers like little orchids
Aesculus carnea, deep red flowers
Aesculus hippocastanum, fl. albo pl., the Baumann horsechestnut with double white flowers.

Larch
Larix laricina, the American larch hackmatack, or tamarack, for its needle tufts and cones.

Mountain Ash
Sorbus aucuparia, for its bright red berries
Sorbus aucuparia, Rowancroft, for bright coral-pink berries.

Tree of Heaven
Ailanthus altissimia, for reddish brown seeds.

VINES

Bittersweet
Celastrus scandens
Celastrus loeseneri, for orange fruit

Clematis
Clematis paniculata, Sweet Autumn Clematis, white fragrant flowers
Clematis virginiana, Virgin's Bower, white flowers in July.

Honeysuckle in variety

Hydrangea
Hydrangea petiolaris, for dainty white flowers.

Silver Lace Vine
Polygonum auberti, for its lacy white flowers in September.

SHRUBS

Alpine Currant
Ribes alpinum, little leaves and greenish yellow flowers.

Barberries in variety
Berberis, for foliage, flower and berry.

Beauty Bush
Kolkwitzia amabilis, for rosy pink flowers in June.

Carolina Allspice
Calycantha floridus, for sweetly scented flowers, brownish.

Cinquefoil in variety
Potentilla fruticosa farreri, leafy twigs.

Daphnes in variety, especially
Daphne Burkwoodi Somerset, for dainty pink, fragrant flowers.

Deutzias in variety, especially
Deutzia gracilis, Pride of Rochester, for double white flowers.

Holly
Ilex verticillata, the Winterberry of our northwoods, for its bright red berries.

Honeysuckle in variety
Lonerica, dainty flowers.

Hydrangeas in variety

Lilacs in variety
Syringa, fragrant clusters of flowers.

Privet in variety
Ligustrum, bunches of glossy blue-black berries.

Russian Olive
Eleagnus angustifolia, for yellow flowers and orange berries.
Eleagnus angustifolia argentea, for silver berries.

Smoketree
Cotinus coggyria, Smoke tree, for foliage.

Snowberry in variety
Symphoricarpos, berries.

Spiraea in variety, especially
Spiraea arguta, with tiny white flowers on black twigs in May.
Spiraea prunifolia flore plena—double white flowers, delightful.

Viburnums in variety, especially
Viburnum fragrans, fragrant flowers in early spring.
Viburnum carlcephalum, a little later.
Viburnum tomentosum rotundifolium, the Japanese Snowball, flowers, especially when they are pale green in the early stage.

Witchhazel in variety, especially
Hamamelis mollis, for fragrant yellow flowers.

PERENNIALS

(Asterisks mark those plants also suitable for miniature gardens)

Alliums in variety
Allium schoenoprasum, chives, good for herb arrangements.

*Androsace Vitaliana
Douglasia Vitaliana, foliage and little yellow flowers.

Artemisia in variety, especially
Artemisia albula, Silver King, for fine gray-white foliage.

Astilbe in variety
Astilbe, foamy flowers in soft colors.

*Baby's Breath
Gypsophila fratensis, clouds of pink flowers.
Gypsophila repens, white flowers.

Barrenwort in variety
Epimedium, perfect flowers for miniatures, white, yellow, deep rose.

*Bellflower
Campanula cochlearifolia alba, tiny leaves and little white bells.
Campanula muralis, dainty blue bells.

Bird's Foot Trefoil
Lotus corniculatus fl. pl., bright yellow flowers.

Black Snakeroot
Cimicifuga racemosa, starry flowers.

Blue-eyed Mary
Omphaloides verna, little flowers, bluer than a forget-me-not.

Candytuft
Iberis sempervirens, Snowflake, dark leaves, snowy white flowers.

Catnip
Nepeta mussini, leaf tips and little flowers.

Coral Bells in variety
Heuchera, little bells in coral, pink and white, perfect scale.

*Chamomile
Anthemis aizoon, silvery foliage and little daisies.

Forget-me-nots in variety
Myosotis, for blue and pink flowers.

Fumitory
Corydalis bulbosa, rosy mauve flowers in early spring.

Grasses in variety, especially
Festuca glauca, the Blue Fescue Grass, a lovely stoney turquoise.

Gromwell
Lithospermum intermedium, little blue bugle flowers.

*Houseleek
Sempervivum, in variety.

Hutchinsia alpine, tiny white flowers.

*Iris
Iris cristata lacustris, our native miniature iris, foliage and flowers.

Jacob's Ladder
Polemonium caeruleum, silvery seeds

Lady's Mantle
Alchemilla alpina, silvery strawberry leaves, good when very small.

Lavender
Lavendula officinalis, fragant blue flower heads.

Lebanon Candytuft
Aethionema pulchellum, Warley Rose, rose pink flowers.

Madwort
Alyssum saxatile, the Golden Tuft of early spring, flowers useful.

Meadowsweet
Filapendula hexapetala, flower heads soft, fluffy white and pink.

Meadow Rue
Thalictrum in variety for foamy flowers.

Primrose
Primula Juliae in variety, for flowers.

Purple Rock Cress
Aubretia, dainty flowers in lavender, purple and pale pink.

Rock Cress in variety, especially
Arabis albida fl. pl., lovely double white flowers.

*Rock Jasmine
Androsace sarmentosa
Androsace sarmentosa chumbyi, foliage and pink flowers both good.

Rock Phlox in variety
Phlox subulata, small foliage and buds of flowers.

*Sandwort
Arenaria caespitosa, lovely moss with tiny flowers.

Savory
Satureja alpina, blue flowers.

*Saxifrages in variety
Saxifraga, nearly all this large family is useful for miniatures

Sea Lavender
Limonium latifolium, minute flowers, dry well.

Snow-in-Summer
Cerastium tomentosum, gray-white foliage.

Spurge
Euphorbia polychroma, bright, chartreuse yellow flowers.

*Stonecrop in variety, especially
Sedum Edwersii, *Sedum glaucum*, *Sedum murale*, *Sedum nevii*, *Sedum reflexum*, all good.

*Thrift in variety
Armeria, little clover heads, pink.

*Thyme
Thymus in variety, for both glossy foliage and good flowers.

*Toad flax
Linaria pallida, tiny lavender flowers.

*Violets in variety, especially
Viola odorata Apricot, a little apricot violet.

*Whitlow Grass
Draba Bertoloni,
Draba bruniaefolia, crisp foliage and excellent yellow flowers.

Yarrow
Achillea tomentosa, gray woolly leaves, yellow flowers.

GREENHOUSE AND FLORIST PLANTS

Babies' Tears
Helxine Soleiroli, soft green foliage, very tiny.

Begonias
Begonia semperflorens, lovely little flowers, doubles particularly good.

Chain Plant

Tradescantia navicularis, miniature, leaves boat shaped, coppery green.

Chlorophytum elatum variegatum, grassy, green and white striped foliage, excellent for line.

Creeping Fig

Ficus pumila minima, small trailing leaves.

Crown of Thorns

Euphorbia splendens, velvety orange or cream flowers, last well.

Gloxinia

Sinningia pusilla, surely one of the littlest plants in captivity!

Ivies in variety, especially

Hedera caenwoodeana, tiny leaves with white veins.
Hedera Needlepoint, tiny, pointed leaves.
Hedera Shamrock, compact, small leaves.
Hedera erecta, small leaves, upright habit.

Kalanchoes in variety

Kalanchoe, starry orange or creamy flowers, last well.

Pomegranate

Punica Granatum, little orange flowers, very dainty.

Strawberry Geranium

Saxifraga sarmentosa, brilliant rosy offshoots.

Succulents and Cacti in variety.

Variegated honeysuckle

Lonerica japonica, variegata, small green and yellow foliage.

Wax Plant

Hoya carnosa, velvety pink flowers, very fragrant

Cuttings of bedding plants like blood leaf, *Iresine Herbsti* or Dusty Miller, *Senecio Cineraria* are good; leaves like Carnation, *Dianthus*, or *Podocarpus* give an interesting line. Small flower heads of Heather, *Erica* are good both fresh and dried.

WILD FLOWERS

(Be sure to check Conservation Lists for your area before picking. Not all parts of every plant listed are correct scale for miniature arrangements. In Solomon Seal, for instance, only the florets would be suitable, in Nightshade, the flowers and berries, but not the leaves.)

Agrimony, *Agrimonia gryposepala*
Bluets, *Houstonia caerulea*
Blue vervain, *Verbena hastata*
Blue Vetch, *Vicia cracca*
Boneset, *Eupatorium perfoliatum*
Buttercup, *Ranunculus acris*
Butter and Eggs, *Linaria vulgaris*
Butterfly weed, *Asclepias tuberosa*
Cardinal flower, *Lobelia cardinalis*
Catnip, *Nepeta cataria*
Celandine,*Chelidonium majus*
Chickweed, *Stellaria media*
Cinquefoil, *Potentilla canadensis*
Creeping Dalibarda, *Dalibarda repens*
False Lily of the Valley, *Maianthemum canadense*
Foam Flower, *Tiarella cordifolia*
Forget-me-not, *Myosotis scorpioides*
Golden rod, *Solidago juncaea*
Goldthread, *Coptis trifolia*
Ground ivy, *Nepeta hederacea*
Hardhack, *Spiraea tomentosa*
Hepatica, *Hepatica triloba*
Herb robert, *Geranium robertianum*
Jewelweed, *Impatiens biflora*
Joe pye weed, *Eupatorium purpureum*
Long-leaved Stitchwort, *Stellaria longifolia*
Lupine, *Lupinus perennis*
Meadow rue, *Thalictrum polyganum*
Meadowsweet, *Spiraea salicifolia*
Milkweed, *Asclepias syriaca*
Mitrewort, *Mitella nuda*
Moneywort, *Lysimachia nummularia*
Mountain laurel, *Kalmia latifolia*
Mustard, *Brassica nigra*
Nightshade, *Solanum dulcamara*
Partridge Berry, *Mitchella repens*
Pearly Everlasting, *Anaphilis margaritacea*
Pimpernel, *Anagallis arvensis*
Pipsissewa, *Chimaphela umbellata*
Queen Anne's Lace, *Daucus carota*
Saxifrage, *Saxifraga virginiensis*
Shinleaf, *Pyrola elliptica*
Silver rod, *Solidago bicolor*
Solomon Seal, *Polygonatum commutatum*
Starflower, *Trientalis americana*
St. Johnswort, *Hypericum perforatum*
Sweet Clover, *Melilotus officinalis*
Tansy, *Tanacetum vulgare*
Toadflax, *Linaria canadensis*
Toothwort, *Dentaria diphylla*
Trailing Arbutus, *Epigaea repens*
Twinflower, *Linnaea borealis americana*
Violet, *Viola* especially *V. pallens*
Virgin's Bower, *Clematis virginiana*
Wild Strawberry, *Fragraria virginiana*
Wintergreen, *Gaultheria procumbens*
Wood Sorrel, *Oxalis corniculata*
Yellow Clover, *Trifolium agrarium*
Club mosses, *Lycopodium*
Ground pine,
Ground cedar,
Seedling ferns and spore cases
Grasses
Seed pods and cones

Appendix B

Plants Suitable for Miniature Landscapes

SMALL-SCALE plants are sometimes difficult to find. We suggest some you might look for. Always check for hardiness in your area, or if you choose tender varieties, plan to move your planting into a cold frame, or cool but not freezing place, for the winter.

EVERGREENS

Buxus, Boxwood, because of the small scale of it leaves, can be trained to a leafy, tree shape. Glossy. All very good.

Buxus microphylla koreana, Korean Box, green turning to warm brown in winter, hardy in severe below-zero weather.

B. suffruticosa Broman, variety of English box, dark green all year.

B. suffructicosa Northland, dwarf, dark green.

Chamaecyparis in variety: although these trees in their natural habitat grow often to one hundred feet, rooted cuttings and juvenile forms are, for the most part, slow-growing, dwarf, and useful for miniature plantings.

Chamaecyparis Lawsoniana Ellwoodi, is compact, conical and has many varieties with different colorings.

Chamaecyparis obtusa, also known in many varieties, most useful being *C. caespitosa*, a bun-like shape three to four inches high;

C. obtusa minima, a dense cushion only a few inches high;

C. obtusa nana, lovely dark green fan-shaped branches, one of the best shapes;

C. obtusa pygmaea, slow-growing, bushy, almost creeping branches.

Chamaecyparis pisifera filifera nana, dense, slender, whip-like branches, the variety *aurea*, the golden one, very good;

C. pisifera plumosa compressa, conical, plumey,

C. pisifera squarrosa pygmaea, dense, soft, golden.

Chamaecyparis thyoides,

C. thyoides andleyensis, erect, purplish in winter.

C. thyoides ericoides, small pyramid, gray-green, purplish in winter.

Cotoneaster dammeri, dwarf cotoneaster, trailing, evergreen, red berries in fall.

Cryptomeria, Japanese Cedar, spreading, conical, branches with pendulous tips.

Cryptomeria japonica, Bandai-sugi, broad, green all winter;

C. elegans nana, plumey, green in summer, bronze in winter;

C. japonica pygmaea, dense pyramidal.

C. vilmoriniana, very dwarf, stunted.

Ericaceae in variety, especially the heathers.

Euonymus radicans minimus (*Kewensis*) dainty, creeping small leaved.

Euonymus radicans variegatus (Silver Gem), small green and white, flushed with pink.

Juniperus in variety: many very hardy through severe winters.

Juniperus communis compressa, slow-growing, erect, cone-shaped

J. horizontalis procumbens, creeping, glaucuous, purplish in winter

J. sabina, Knap Hill, low, dense, plumey, bright green

J. chinensis blauuwi, upright, neat, intense green, very good

J. chinensis obelisk, compact, pyramid, bluish, neat

J. chinensis skandia, flat, compact, greyish blue

J. virginiana nova, compact, symmetrical, purplish in winter

J. coxi, graceful, slender trunk, often pendulous.

Picea in variety

Picea abies nidiformis, Nest Spruce, forms a low, dense pincushion.

P. abies glauca conica, Dwarf White Spruce, a very slow growing, compact, pyramid, with grassy, green needles.

P. abies albertiana, Alberta Spruce, slow growing, dense, conical, bright green.

P. abies clanbrasiliana, dense, slow-growing, bushy.

P. abies dumosa, dense, slow-growing, short branches.

P. abies echiniformis, very dwarf, flat topped.

P. abies pygmaea, very slow-growing, dense.

Thuja occidentalis nana (Little Gem), Northern White Cedar very dwarf, slow-growing.

Veronica decumbens, shiny, purple-black shoots, white flowers.

PERENNIALS

Suggested varieties for miniature plantings are marked with an asterisk in the list of perennials for miniature flower arrangements on pages 159–161. Others you may find in nursery catalogs for your area, especially those specializing in plants for rock gardens.

BULBS

Many miniature bulbs, with flowers suitable for plantings, tend to become clumsy and untidy after blooming. We suggest that they be lifted carefully after flowering and heeled in somewhere else to ripen, stored, and then planted again for the next season, or grown in a small pot which can be buried to its rim in the planting, and later removed.

Chionodoxa, Glory of the Snow, var. *Luciliae*, bright blue white centre.

Chionodoxa Luciliae rosea, pink.

C. Sardensis, true gentian blue, white centre.

C. Tmoli, small, blue and white, very late.

Crocus species, in variety. (The species are smaller than other crocus), especially

Crocus Ancyrensis, rare, early, orange, free flowering.

C. Aureus sulphureus concolor, soft lemon yellow.

C. chrysanthus, Blue Pearl, new, delicate silvery blue.

C. chrysanthus, Snow Bunting, white, gold throat, exterior purplish.

C. Tomasinianus, Whitewell Purple, reddish purple.

Cyclamen, miniatures of familiar greenhouse varieties.

Cyclamen Libanoticum, rare, white, spring flowering.

C. neapolitanum (Ivy-leaved Cyclamen) rosy pink, autumn flowering.

Galanthus (Snowdrops) Avoid newer varieties, they are too big.
Galanthus nivalis, common snowdrop.
G. nivalis plenus, double form.

Hyacinthus, Alpine Hyacinth
Hyacinthus amethystinus, amethyst blue, late spring.
H. amethystinus alba, white form.

Muscari (Grape Hyacinths) spikey flowers of early spring. Choose smaller varieties especially,
Muscari argaei album, small, white bells on tapering stock.
M. acureum, bright blue, early.
M. armeniacum cantab, new bright blue, short.

Narcissus (Daffodils) These are the species.
Narcissus bulbocodium, (The Hoop Petticoat Daffodil), golden yellow, trumpet like a petticoat.
N. cyclamineus, reflexed, clear yellow.
N. helena gracilis, late, sweet-scented, sulphur yellow.
N. juncifolius, baby jonquil, rush leaves, tiny, very fragrant.
N. minimus, the smallest of all, hardy in Zone 4.
N. nanus, white and yellow.
N. juncifolius rupicola, bright yellow, graceful.
N. scaberulus, rare, deep yellow with orange toned cup, tiny.
N. triandus albus, Angel's Tears, white, bell-shaped, clustered. Lovely.
N. watieri, rare, tiny, pure white.

Scilla sibirica, bright blue, early.
Scilla sibirica alba, same form in white.
S. bifolia rosea, rare, early, pink.

Appendix C

Miniature Roses

ALTHOUGH more than 150 varieties of miniature roses are being grown today, not all of them are easily available nor suitable for all garden conditions. Our list is made up of varieties which have been successfully grown in Zone 4 (the southwest part of the province of Ontario in Canada and Northern New York State) and the best of some of the new varieties that are worth trying. If you are interested in more of them, send for catalogues of the nurseries listed in Appendix E.

Baby Darling	coral apricot; low-spreading
Baby Masquerade	unusual color—yellow aging to pink, then red—fine, upright plant
Bo-Peep	pale pink; glossy green leaves
Cinderella	shell pink shading to white; free-flowering; one of the best; good for arrangements
Colibri	low-spreading; lovely yellow-to-orange bloom; fully double
Coralin	coral pink shaded with flame; small, lovely form; one of the best
Dwarfking	dark red long-lasting flowers; tallish

Easter Morning	white; hybrid tea-form in bud; upright bush
Eleanor	coral pink; exquisite
For You (Pour Toi)	white; upright; excellent for arrangements
Granadina	oxblood red
Jeanie Williams	red and yellow bicolor like a miniature Talisman rose
Mary Adair	apricot; dainty hybrid tea-form blossoms
Midget	small red flowers in clusters
Perla de Alcanada	crimson; free-blooming; erect, bushy plant; good for arrangements
Perla de Montserrat	one of the best; rose pink; hybrid tea-form buds; excellent for arrangements
Pixie	a real fairy rose; low-spreading bush; seldom exceeds six inches in height; flowers white flushed with pink
Pixie Gold	small golden yellow flowers; petite foliage
Red Imp	very small dark red double blossoms in clusters
Robin	red aging to dark pink flowers; one of the best; sturdy, compact, and upright; tightly quilled petals
Scarlet Gem	bright red; flower like a miniature dahlia; petals tipped black
Simple Simon	deep pink; extremely dwarf; exquisite and excellent for arrangements
Sweet Fairy	apple-blossom pink; very free blooming; fragrant; bushy in the open; a tendency to climb if planted against a wall or rock
Tom Thumb	low-spreading; one of the oldest but still good; red with a white eye; cup-shaped; semidouble flowers
Yellow Doll	the best yellow; lovely in bud; fades to white when open

NEWER VARIETIES

Beauty Secret	hybrid tea-form red; opens to show yellow stamens
Chipper	large bush; coral-red flowers
Fairy Moss	pink, with moss-rose sepals
Lavender Lace	a true lavender blue
Starina	coral red; exceptional

Appendix D

Miniature Geraniums

(average height, 2-3 inches)

VARIETIES WITH SINGLE BLOOMS

Alcyone	bright pink
Brownie	scarlet; leaves marked with brown
Fairy Tales	large ruffled white with lavender center; dark-zoned leaves
North Star	white; veined pink
Pixie	salmon-pink; dark foliage
Polaris	white with pink edge
Red Comet	scarlet with white center; green leaves
Rober's Lavender	large lavender-pink flowers
Salmon Comet	salmon; black-zoned leaf; small-flowered
Sirius	small pink flower; blooms freely
Stormy	dark red flowers; dark leaf
Tiny Tim	tiny pink or red flowers; small-scale leaves
Vixen	fine salmon-pink
Zip	narrow-petaled red; black-zoned leaf

VARIETIES WITH DOUBLE BLOOMS

Capella	light salmon; dark foliage

Goblin	bright red; largish flowers
Heide	pink; apple-blossom type
Merope	dark red; dark leaves
Minx	purple-crimson; ruffled leaves
Mischief	orange-red; cactus-type petals
Pigmy	bright red; semidouble
Rocket	purple-vermilion; dark leaves
Rosy Dawn	salmon orange-red; dark leaves
Ruffles	light salmon; semidouble; small-flowered
Saturn	bright scarlet; flowers well
Small Fortune	white shading to pink; bushy
Trinket	salmon-apricot

SCENTED, VARIEGATED, AND IVY-LEAVED

Pelargonium crispum	lemon-scented; grows like a tiny evergreen
Prince Rupert	lemon-scented; variegated chartreuse; green and cream ruffled leaves; excellent for miniatures
P. odoratissimum	small leaves; apple-scented
L'Elegante (Sunset)	small, ivy-leaved variety; leaves green, grayish, and sometimes flushed with pink; flowers not miniature
Gay Baby	trailing, tiny ivy leaves; white flowers; constant bloom
Sugar Baby	as above, with pink flowers; spring to late fall bloom

Appendix E

Where to Buy Miniature Plants and Seeds, Figurines, and Supplies

Name and Address	Cost of Catalog	Specialty
Alpenglow Gardens 13328 Trans-Canada Highway North Surrey, P.O. New Westminster, British Columbia, Canada	Free	Alpine, evergreens, shrubs
Alva Museum Replicas, Inc. 30-30 Northern Boulevard Long Island City, New York 11101	Free	Authentic replicas of museum sculptures
Buell, Albert H. Eastford, Connecticut 06242	\$1.00 (Handbook)	Gesneriads
Cruickshank Limited, C. A. 1015 Mount Pleasant Road Toronto 12, Canada	Free	Seeds, roses, bulbs
de Jager and Sons, Inc., P. 188 Asbury Street South Hamilton, Massachusetts 01982	Free	Bulbs, miniature gladiolus

Name and Address	Cost of Catalog	Specialty
Dolbow, Dorothy J. Penns Grove, New Jersey 08069	Free	Supplies, equipment
Girard Nurseries Geneva, Ohio 44041	Free	Trees and shrubs
Hopper, Lois 3940 Oak Street Kansas City, Missouri 64111	Free	African violets (no shipping)
House Plant Corner, The P. O. Box 810 Oxford, Maryland 21654	20¢	Supplies, equipment
Kartuz, Michael J. 92 Chestnut Street Wilmington, Massachusetts 01887	25¢	African violets, begonias, gesneriads
Logee's Greenhouses 55 North Street Danielson, Connecticut 06239	50¢	Begonias, geraniums, rare plants
McConnell's Nursery Port Burwell, Ontario, Canada	Free	Roses
Merry Gardens Camden, Maine 04843	$1.20 (Handbook)	Begonias, geraniums, ivies, others
Mini-Roses P. O. Box 4255 Station A Dallas, Texas 75208	Free	Miniature roses
Park Company, Geo. W. Greenwood, South Carolina 29646	Free	Seeds, supplies, equipment, bulbs
Pinehaven Nurseries Limited 475 Queensway West Mississuaga, Ontario, Canada	Free	Miniature roses
Robin, Clyde P. O. Box 2091 Castro Valley, California 94546	50¢	Extensive—native plants, roses, seeds
Roehrs Company, Julius Rutherford, New Jersey	10¢	Plants

Name and Address	Cost of Catalog	Specialty
Saier, Harry Dimondale, Michigan 48821	50¢	Seeds
Sequoia Nursery (Mr. Ralph Moore) 2519 East Noble Avenue Visalia, California 93277	Free	Roses—bush, tree, and climbing miniatures
Sky-Cleft Garden Camp Street Extension Barre, Vermont 05641	10¢	Alpines
Tropical Paradise Greenhouse 8825 West 79 Street Overland Park, Kansas 66204	50¢	Begonias, cacti, succulents, ferns (no shipping)
Wyant, Melvin E. Rose Specialist, Inc. 200 Johnny Cake Ridge Mentor, Ohio 44060	Free	Roses

Index

Lois Wilson, of Toronto, Canada, is a free-lance writer on gardening, flower arranging, and the folkways and foibles of everyday living. She is Garden Editor of *Chatelaine* magazine, the author of *Chatelaine's Gardening Book*, and coauthor of *Flowers for Your Church*. Her articles frequently appear in national gardening magazines, and she has written the authoritative material on "Western Flower Arrangement" for the *Encyclopedia Americana*.

A distinguished arranger in both full scale and miniature, Mrs. Wilson has won many first ribbons and holds the Founders' Gold Cup of The Garden Club of Toronto, of which she is a past president. In her leisure time she hunts for wild flowers, gardens, travels, and is an avid collector of miniature containers and accessories.

Lois Wilson is a Regent of Victoria University of the University of Toronto, a member of the National Council of the Canadian Institute for the Blind, and a recipient in 1967 of Canada's Centennial Medal for valuable service to the nation.